PRIDE & PREJU~KNITS

A RotoVision book

Published in 2015 by Search Press Ltd.
Wellwood, North Farm Road
Tunbridge Wells
Kent, TN2 3DR

This book is produced by
RotoVision SA, Sheridan House, 114 Western Road
Hove, BN3 1DD

ISBN 978-1-78221-313-0

Publisher: Mark Searle
Editorial Director: Isheeta Mustafi
Commissioning Editor: Alison Morris
Assistant Editor: Tamsin Richardson
Editor: Cath Senker
Art Director: Michelle Rowlandson
Layout: Kate Haynes and Richard Peters
Cover design: Agata Rybicka
Prop and background design: Agata Rybicka
Photography: Volfgang Knipsen
Illustrations: Rob Brandt and Agata Rybicka

PRIDE & PREJU~KNITS

12 GENTEEL KNITTING PROJECTS
INSPIRED BY JANE AUSTEN

TRIXIE VON PURL

SEARCH PRESS

CONTENTS

LYDIA
Pride and Prejudice

VICAR
Emma

MARIANNE
Sense and Sensibility

CAPTAIN WENTWORTH
Persuasion

FANNY
Mansfield Park

CATHERINE
Northanger Abbey

How to use this book

What a dream it's been to re-create these scenes from Jane Austen's finest moments! In a market swamped by film and TV adaptations, it's not until you look closely at the original text that you realise how funny and sharp that lady must have been in person. Having said that, one of the reasons those Austen adaptations are so popular is the way that they bring the wonderful costumes and locations to life. I hope, in its own humble way, that this book adds a tiny stitched visual contribution to the plethora of interpretations.

This is not the average knitting book and the projects require a little more patience and attention than regular children's dolls knitted in DK yarns, but I hope you'll agree that the results make them worthwhile. The figures themselves are knitted in 4ply yarn on fine needles in the round, which helps to give them shaping and detail. The clothing and objects explore different stitches and techniques, so for those knitters who get bored easily with simple projects and who enjoy a challenge, this book is definitely for you! Inside these pages you'll find lacework, colourwork and short row shaping, among more straightforward stitches and techniques. If you'd like to check the complexity of the patterns, look at the Abbreviations (page 110) and Basic Techniques (pages 20–21) sections and read through the patterns carefully before picking up your needles.

It is, of course, the hair and facial features that give the dolls their personality. The facial features are similar on every character, but it's amazing what a difference a stern stitched brow, an unsmiling mouth or different-coloured eyes here and there can make. You can even suggest whether a character has enjoyed a few too many rich meals by adjusting the amount of stuffing in the doll (I'm looking at you, Sir Thomas, with your portly tummy on page 100).

The male dolls are knitted on a larger-size needle than the ladies, making them slightly bigger – although you can choose to knit the ladies the same size by using the same needles recommended for the gents. If you do so, remember that you will need to make a similar needle-size adjustment to knit the accompanying garments.

The dolls contain wire to make them flexible. I've used armature wire (the strong, flexible model-maker's wire of choice), but you could also use florist's wire or strong pipe cleaners if you prefer. Of course, you don't have to use wire at all if you're not going to pose the dolls, but it does make for endless possibilities!

On pages 8–14 you'll find the basic doll patterns, and on pages 20–21 there are instructions for the basic techniques; extra techniques are explained on page 108. Many of the patterns, such as the Gentlemen's Boots, Ladies' Shoes and the Breeches, are repeated throughout. You will find them in a handy section entitled Knitting Regency Outfits on pages 16–19.

YARN
Each pattern has a Materials section with yarn suggestions, but feel free to experiment because these projects make ideal stash-busters. If you are replacing yarns, make sure you use a yarn of the same weight as the original suggestion. Some projects use a very small amount of a particular colour that doesn't necessitate buying a whole ball, in which case the pattern will read 'Small amount of xxx yarn,' and you may be able to use yarn from your stash. Most of the patterns have a tension guide. If this were a life-size garment book I'd tell you to stick rigidly to this and always knit a tension swatch, but here we can afford to be a little more relaxed – the items are small, so any differences in tension won't be obvious in the finished outcome. Where there is no tension guide, the finished size does not have to be exact.

STRUCTURES
Some of the items use cardboard and/or foam as an interior structure to support the knitting (for instance, the Pianoforte on page 89, and the Armchair on page 27). Where there is a shape involved, I have included a template for you to copy, whereas the simpler patterns will give you the dimensions to work to. All of the materials required are easy to find, either around the home or from craft and hardware shops.

So, Austen fans, go forth and knit, and may all your figures be possessed of the same wit and charm with which Jane Austen originally infused them!

KNITTING REGENCY LADIES

MATERIALS

Yarn in the following options:

- 1 x 50g ball Debbie Bliss Rialto 4ply (fingering 100% wool; 50g/196yds) in shade 034 Blush OR shade 038 Mink

OR

- 1 x 50g ball King Cole Merino Blend 4ply (fingering 100% wool; 50g/196yds) in shade 790 Caramel OR shade 929 Fudge
- Small amounts of yarn in preferred colour for hair, eyes and mouth
- Set of 5 x 2.75mm (US 2) dpns
- 6 stitch holders
- 8 pipe cleaners, 30cm long x 6mm thick (12 x ¼in)

TENSION

Approx. 30 sts and 48 rows = 10cm (4in) over St-st.

FINISHED MEASUREMENTS

Approx. 29cm (11½in) from head to heel

PATTERN NOTE: The doll is knitted in rounds from the toes up. The arms and legs are made separately using 4 dpns and then joined into the torso as it is worked on 5 dpns. Stuff the doll and add pipe cleaners where indicated (see page 21 for stuffing tips).

LEGS (MAKE 2)
FOOT
With 2 dpns, cast on 3 sts.
Next row: Kfb into each st (6 sts).
Slip 2 sts on to each of 3 dpns. Place a marker at beg of rnd. Work in rnds from now on.
Rnd 1: K.
Rnd 2: (Kfb) 3 times, k2, kfb (10 sts).
Rnd 3: K.
Rnd 4: Kfb, k2, (kfb) twice, k4, kfb (14 sts).
Rnd 5: K.
Rnd 6: Kfb, k4, (kfb) twice, k6, kfb (18 sts).
There should now be 8 sts on needle 1 (sole of foot), and 5 sts each on needles 2 and 3 (foot top).
Rnds 7–16: K.
SHAPE HEEL
The heel is worked on 8 sts on needle 1 only (work back and forth instead of in rnds).
Row 1: K7, w&t.
Row 2: P6, w&t.
Row 3: K5, w&t.
Row 4: P4, w&t.
Row 5: K3, w&t.
Row 6: P2, w&t.
Row 7: K3, working wrap into st, turn.
Row 8: P4, turn.
Row 9: K5, turn.
Row 10: P6, turn.

Row 11: K7, turn.
Row 12: P8.
ANKLE AND CALF
Beg working in rnds again:
Rnd 1: K8 from needle 1, pick up yarn strand lying between last st knitted and next st on needle 2, sl on to needle 2 and k tog with next st (this closes gap between heel and foot). K to end.
Rnd 2: Pick up yarn strand lying between last st knitted and first st on needle 1, sl on to needle 1 and k tog with next st (this closes gap between heel and foot). K to end.
Rnds 3–6: K.
Rnd 7: K1, skpo, k2, k2tog, k to end (16 sts).
Rnds 8–15: K.
Rnd 16: K2, m1R, k2, m1L, k to end (18 sts).
Rnds 17–18: K.
Rnd 19: K1, m1R, k6, m1L, k to end (20 sts).
Rnds 20–29: K.
KNEE
Rnd 1: K1, skpo, k4, k2tog, k to end (18 sts).
Rnds 2–3: K.
Rnd 4: K1, skpo, k2, k2tog, k to end (16 sts).
Rnd 5: K1, skpo, k2tog, k3, m1R, k6, m1L, k2 (16 sts).
Rnd 6: K6, m1R, k8, m1L, k2 (18 sts).
Rnd 7: K6, m1R, k10, m1L, k2 (20 sts).
Rnds 8–9: K.
Rnd 10: K6, skpo, k8, k2tog, k2 (18 sts).
Rnd 11: K1, m1R, k2, m1L, k3, skpo, k6, k2tog, k2 (18 sts).
Rnd 12: K8, skpo, k4, k2tog, k2 (16 sts).
THIGH
Rnd 1: K1, m1R, k4, m1L, k to end (18 sts).

1

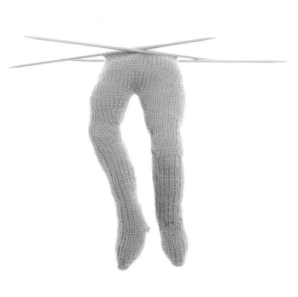

2

3

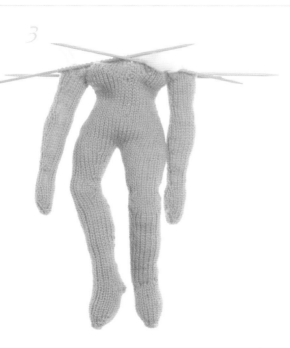

4

Rnd 2: K1, m1R, k6, m1L, k2, m1R, k8, m1L, k1 (22 sts).

Rnds 3–5: K.

Rnd 6: K1, m1R, k8, m1L, k2, m1R, k10, m1L, k1 (26 sts).

Rnds 7–11: K.

Rnd 12: K1, m1R, k10, m1L, k2, m1R, k12, m1L, k1 (30 sts).

Rnd 13: K1, m1R, k to end (31 sts).

Rnds 14–23: K.

Slip 15 sts from needle 1 on to first st-holder (this will be the back of the leg), 16 sts from needles 2 and 3 on to second st-holder (this will be the front of the leg – see illus. 1).

TORSO
JOIN LEGS
Use 4 dpns. With RS facing, slip 16 sts of front of first leg on to needle 1, 16 sts of front of second leg on to needle 2, 15 sts of back of second leg on to needle 3, 15 sts of back of first leg on to needle 4 (62 sts). Place a marker for beg of rnd. Rejoin yarn, k 1 rnd (see illus. 2).

BUTTOCKS
Rnd 1: K14, p1, k2, p1, k to end.

Rnd 2: K13, p1, k4, p1, k16, m1R, k9, m1L, k6, m1R, k9, m1L, k3 (66 sts).

Rnd 3: Skpo, k10, p1, k6, p1, k10, k2tog, skpo, k1, m1R, k11, m1L, k2, k2tog, k2, m1R, k11, m1L, k1, k2tog (65 sts).

Rnd 4: K10, p1, k8, p1, k to end.

Rnd 5: Skpo, k7, p1, k10, p1, k7, k2tog, skpo, m1R, k14, m1L, k1, k2tog, m1R, k14, m1L, k2tog (64 sts).

Rnd 6: K.

Rnd 7: Skpo, k24, k2tog, skpo, m1R, k14, m1L, k2tog, skpo, m1R, k14, m1L, k2tog (62 sts).

Rnd 8: K.

SHAPE WAIST
Rnd 9: Skpo, k22, k2tog, skpo, k to last 2 sts, k2tog (58 sts).

Rnd 10: K.

Rnd 11: Skpo, k20, k2tog, (skpo) twice, k11, k2tog, skpo, k11, (k2tog) twice (50 sts).

Rnd 12: K.

Rnd 13: Skpo, k18, k2tog, (skpo) twice, k8, k2tog, skpo, k8, (k2tog) twice (42 sts).

Rnd 14: K.

Rnd 15: K22, skpo, k3, k2tog, k4, skpo, k3, k2tog, k2 (38 sts).

Rnd 16: K20, skpo, k14, k2tog (36 sts).

Rnd 17: K21, skpo, k1, k2tog, k4, skpo, k1, k2tog, k1 (32 sts).

Rnd 18: Skpo, k16, k2tog, skpo, k to last 2 sts, k2tog (28 sts).

Rnd 19: K20, m1R, k1, m1L, k4, m1R, k1, m1L, k2 (32 sts).

Rnd 20: K1, m1R, k16, m1L, k2, m1R, k to last st, m1L, k1 (36 sts).

Rnd 21: K24, m1R, k3, m1L, k4, m1R, k3, m1L, k2 (40 sts).

Rnd 22: (K1, m1R, k18, m1L, k1) twice (44 sts).

Rnd 23: K.

Rnd 24: (K1, m1R, k20, m1L, k1) twice (48 sts).

Rnd 25: K.

Rnd 26: (K1, m1R, k22, m1L, k1) twice (52 sts).

Rnd 27: K.

Rnd 28: K1, m1R, k24, m1L, k to end (54 sts).

SHAPE BREASTS
Each breast is worked separately. The chest sts are divided into two sections of 14 sts each, which are shaped with short rows.

Row 1: K13, w&t.

Row 2: P12, w&t.

Row 3: K11, w&t.

Row 4: P10, w&t.

Row 5: K9, w&t.

Row 6: P8, w&t.

Row 7: K7, w&t.

Row 8: P6, w&t.

Row 9: K5, w&t.

Row 10: P4, w&t.

Row 11: K3, w&t.

Row 12: P2, w&t.

Row 13: K8, turn, working wraps into sts.

Row 14: P14, turn, working wraps into sts.

Cut yarn and rejoin to 14 sts on needle 2 for second breast. Rep rows 1 to 14, ending at centre of chest. Cut yarn. With RS facing, rejoin yarn to beg of rnd, k across 28 sts of chest. Cut yarn. With RS facing, rejoin yarn to beg of needle 3, k across 26 sts of back, turn.

Next row: P26, turn.

Next row: K26 to end of row.

Next row: Cast off 2 sts, k24, cast off 4 sts, k22 to last 2 sts, cast off last 2 sts.

Slip 24 sts from chest on to first st-holder and 22 sts from back on to second st-holder. Sew gap between legs.

STUFFING STAGE 1
See page 21.

ARMS (MAKE 2)
HAND
With 2 dpns, cast on 3 sts.

Next row: Kfb into each st (6 sts). Slip 2 sts on to each of 3 dpns. Place a marker at beg of rnd.

Rnd 1: K.

Rnd 2: (Kfb, k2) twice (8 sts).

Rnd 3: K.

Rnd 4: (Kfb, k3) twice (10 sts).

Rnd 5: K.

Rnd 6: (Kfb, k4) twice (12 sts).

Rnd 7: K.

Rnd 8: (Kfb, k5) twice (14 sts).

Rnds 9–10: K.

Rnd 11: (Skpo, k5) twice (12 sts).

Rnd 12: K.

Rnd 13: (Skpo, k4) twice (10 sts).

WRIST AND FOREARM
Rnds 14–18: K.

Rnd 19: (K1, m1R, k4) twice
(12 sts).
Rnds 20–24: K.
Rnd 25: (K1, m1R, k5) twice
(14 sts).
Sl last 2 sts from needle 2 on to beg
of needle 3.
Rnds 26–30: K.
Rnd 31: (K1, m1R, k6) twice
(16 sts).
Rnds 32–36: K.
Rnd 37: (Skpo, k6) twice
(14 sts).
Rnd 38: K.
Rnd 39: (Skpo, k5) twice
(12 sts).
Rnds 40–43: K.
UPPER ARMS
Rnd 44: (K1, m1R, k5) twice
(14 sts).
Rnds 45–46: K.
Rnd 47: (K1, m1R, k6) twice
(16 sts).
Rnds 48–50: K.
Rnd 51: (K1, m1R, k7) twice
(18 sts).
Rnds 52–54: K.
Rnd 55: (K1, m1R, k8) twice
(20 sts).
Rnd 56: K.
Rnd 57: (K1, m1R, k9) twice
(22 sts).
Rnd 58: K.
Rnd 59: (K1, m1R, k10) twice
(24 sts).
Rnd 60: K4, cast off 4 sts, k16
(20 sts).
Beg at gap of cast-off sts, slip 10 sts
on to first st-holder and 10 sts on to
second st-holder. Cast-off sts form
the armpit.

UPPER CHEST

The arms are now joined to the
torso. Lay the torso flat with the
chest uppermost. Place an arm on
each side with the armpit cast-off sts
facing towards the torso. Slip sts for
arms and torso from st-holders on to
4 dpns as follows (see illus. 3):
Needle 1: 10 sts from front of left

arm and 12 sts from left chest
(22 sts).
Needle 2: Rem 12 sts from right
chest and 10 sts from front of right
arm (22 sts).
Turn doll so back is uppermost.
Needle 3: Rem 10 sts from right
arm and 11 sts from right back
(21 sts).
Needle 4: Rem 11 sts from left back
and rem 10 sts from left arm
(21 sts). (86 sts in total)
Place a marker for beg of rnd.
Rejoin yarn to start of needle 1
(front of left arm) and cont in rnds
as follows:
Rnd 1: K.
Rnd 2: K8, k2tog, skpo, k20, k2tog,
skpo, k16, k2tog, k22, skpo, k8
(80 sts).
Rnd 3: K.
Rnd 4: (K7, k2tog, skpo, k18, k2tog,
skpo, k7) twice (72 sts).
Rnd 5: K.
Leave sts on needles but make sure
sts cannot slip off (use point
protectors or similar).
STUFFING STAGE 2
See page 21.

Rnd 6: (K6, k2tog, skpo, k16, k2tog,
skpo, k6) twice (64 sts).
Rnd 7: K.
Rnd 8: (K5, k2tog, skpo, k14, k2tog,
skpo, k5) twice (56 sts).
Rnd 9: K.
Rnd 10: (K4, k2tog, skpo, k12,
k2tog, skpo, k4) twice (48 sts).
Rnd 11: K.
Rnd 12: (K3, k2tog, skpo, k10,
k2tog, skpo, k3) twice (40 sts).
Rnd 13: K.
Rnd 14: (K2, k2tog, skpo, k8, k2tog,
skpo, k2) twice (32 sts).
Rnd 15: K.
Rnd 16: (K1, k2tog, skpo, k6, k2tog,
skpo, k1) twice (24 sts).
Stuff chest firmly.
Rnd 17: K.
Rnd 18: (K2tog, skpo, k4, k2tog,
skpo) twice (16 sts).
Rnd 19: K.

NECK AND HEAD

Rnds 1–4: K.
Rnd 5: (K1, kfb) 8 times (24 sts).
Rnd 6: K.
Rnd 7: (K2, kfb) 8 times (32 sts).
Rnd 8: K.
Rnd 9: (K3, kfb) 8 times (40 sts).
Rnd 10: K.
Rnd 11: (K4, kfb) 8 times (48 sts).
Rnds 12–14: K.
Rnd 15: K10, kfb, k37 (49 sts).
Rnd 16 (make the nose): K11, (kfb)
twice into next st, turn, p4, turn,
(k2tog) twice, turn, p2tog, turn, k
to end of rnd.
Rnd 17: K11, k2tog, k to end
(48 sts).
Rnds 18–20: K.
Rnd 21: (K4, k2tog) 8 times
(40 sts).
Rnd 22: K.
Rnd 23: (K3, k2tog) 8 times
(32 sts).
Rnd 24: K.
Rnd 25: (K2, k2tog) 8 times
(24 sts).
Stuff the neck and head firmly.
Rnd 26: (K1, k2tog) 8 times
(16 sts).
Rnd 27: K.
Rnd 28: (K2tog) 8 times (8 sts).
Rnd 29: K.
Rnd 30: (K2tog) 4 times (4 sts).
Stuff the head.
Cut yarn, leaving a long end, thread
through rem sts, pull up tightly and
secure yarn end.

MAKING UP

See page 20 to add facial features,
hair, and other details to
personalise your doll (see illus. 4).

KNITTING REGENCY GENTLEMEN

MATERIALS

Yarn in the following options:

- 1 x 50g ball Debbie Bliss Rialto 4ply (100% wool; 50g/201yds) in shade 034 Blush OR shade 038 Mink

OR

- 1 x 50g ball King Cole Merino Blend 4ply (100% wool; 50g/201yds) in shade 790 Caramel

OR

- 1 x 100g ball King Cole Big Value 4ply (100% acrylic; 100g/448yds) in shade 677 Dune
- Set of 5 x 3.25mm (US 3) dpns
- 6 stitch holders
- 2 point protectors
- 8 pipe cleaners or armature wire 30cm long x 6mm thick (12 x ¼in)

TENSION

Approx. 30 sts and 48 rows = 10cm (4in) over St-st.

FINISHED MEASUREMENTS

Approx. 33cm (13in) from head to heel

PATTERN NOTE: The doll is knitted in rounds from the toes up. The arms and legs are made separately using 4 dpns and then joined into the torso as it is worked on 5 dpns. Stuff the doll and add pipe cleaners where indicated (see page 21 for stuffing tips).

LEGS (MAKE 2)
FOOT
With 2 dpns, cast on 3 sts.
Next row: Kfb into each st (6 sts). Slip 2 sts on to each of 3 dpns. Place a marker at beg of rnd. Work in rnds from now on.
Rnd 1: K.
Rnd 2: (Kfb) 3 times, k2, kfb (10 sts).
Rnd 3: K.
Rnd 4: Kfb, k2, (kfb) twice, k4, kfb (14 sts).
Rnd 5: K.
Rnd 6: Kfb, k4, (kfb) twice, k6, kfb (18 sts).
There should now be 8 sts on needle 1 (sole of foot), and 5 sts each on needles 2 and 3 (foot top).
Rnds 7–16: K.
SHAPE HEEL
The heel is worked on 8 sts on needle 1 only (work back and forth instead of in rnds).
Row 1: K7, w&t.
Row 2: P6, w&t.
Row 3: K5, w&t.
Row 4: P4, w&t.
Row 5: K3, w&t.
Row 6: P2, w&t.
Row 7: K3, working wrap into st, turn.
Row 8: P4, turn.

Row 9: K5, turn.
Row 10: P6, turn.
Row 11: K7, turn.
Row 12: P8.
ANKLE AND CALF
Beg working in rnds again.
Rnd 1: K8 from needle 1, pick up yarn strand lying between last st knitted and next st on needle 2, sl on to needle 2 and k tog with next st (this closes gap between heel and foot). K to end.
Rnd 2: Pick up yarn strand lying between last st knitted and first st on needle 1, sl on to needle 1 and k tog with next st (this closes gap between heel and foot). K to end.
Rnds 3–6: K.
Rnd 7: K1, skpo, k2, k2tog, k to end (16 sts).
Rnds 8–15: K.
Rnd 16: K2, m1R, k2, m1L, k to end (18 sts).
Rnds 17–18: K.
Rnd 19: K1, m1R, k6, m1L, k to end (20 sts).
Rnds 20–29: K.
KNEE
Rnd 1: K1, skpo, k4, k2tog, k to end (18 sts).
Rnds 2–3: K.
Rnd 4: K1, skpo, k2, k2tog, k to end (16 sts).
Rnd 5: K1, skpo, k2tog, k3, m1R, k6, m1L, k2 (16 sts).
Rnd 6: K6, m1R, k8, m1L, k2 (18 sts).
Rnd 7: K6, m1R, k10, m1L, k2 (20 sts).
Rnds 8–9: K.
Rnd 10: K6, skpo, k8, k2tog, k2 (18 sts).
Rnd 11: K1, m1R, k2, m1L, k3, skpo, k6, k2tog, k2 (18 sts).
Rnd 12: K8, skpo, k4, k2tog, k2 (16 sts).

THIGH

Rnd 1: K1, m1R, k4, m1L, k to end (18 sts).
Rnd 2: K1, m1R, k6, m1L, k2, m1R, k8, m1L, k1 (22 sts).
Rnds 3–5: K.
Rnd 6: K1, m1R, k8, m1L, k2, m1R, k10, m1L, k1 (26 sts).
Rnds 7–11: K.
Rnd 12: K1, m1R, k10, m1L, k2, m1R, k12, m1L, k1 (30 sts).
Rnds 13–22: K.
Slip 15 sts from needle 1 on to first st-holder (this will be the back of the leg), 15 sts from needles 2 and 3 on to second st-holder (this will be the front of the leg).

TORSO
JOIN LEGS
Use 4 dpns. With RS facing, slip 15 sts of front of first leg on to needle 1, 15 sts of front of second leg on to needle 2, 15 sts of back of second leg on to needle 3, 15 sts of back of first leg on to needle 4 (60 sts). Place a marker for beg of rnd.
Rnd 1: K (60 sts).
Rnd 2: K34, m1R, k8, m1L, k6, m1R, k8, m1L, k4 (64 sts).
Rnd 3: Skpo, k26, k2tog, (skpo) twice, m1R, k10, m1L, k2, k2tog, k2, m1R, k10, m1L, (k2tog) twice (61 sts).
Rnd 4: K.
Rnd 5: Skpo, k24, k2tog, skpo, k2, m1R, k10, m1L, k1, k2tog, k2, m1R, k10, m1L, k2, k2tog (60 sts).
Rnd 6: K.
Rnd 7: Skpo, k22, k2tog, skpo, k1, m1R, k12, m1L, k1, k2tog, k1, m1R, k12, m1L, k1, k2tog (59 sts).
Rnd 8: K.
Rnd 9: K24, k2tog, m1R, k14, m1L, k3, m1R, k14, m1L, k2tog (61 sts).
Rnd 10: K.
Rnd 11: K24, k1, skpo, k12, k2tog, k1, k2tog, skpo, k12, k2tog, k1 (56 sts).
Rnd 12: K.
Rnd 13: Kfb, k22, kfb into next 2 sts, skpo, k10, k2tog, k2, skpo, k10,

k2tog, kfb (56 sts).
Rnd 14: K.
Rnd 15: Kfb, k24, kfb twice, k1, skpo, k8, k2tog, k2, skpo, k8, k2tog, k1, kfb (56 sts).
Rnd 16: K.
Rnd 17: Kfb, k26, kfb into next 2 sts, k2, skpo, k6, k2tog, k2, skpo, k6, k2tog, k2, kfb (56 sts).
Rnd 18: K.
Rnd 19: Kfb, k28, kfb, k4, skpo, k3, k2tog, k4, skpo, k3, k2tog, k4 (54 sts).
Rnd 20: K.
Rnd 21: K32, kfb, k3, skpo, k1, k2tog, k4, skpo, k1, k2tog, k3, kfb (52 sts).
Rnd 22: K.
Rnd 23: K38, (m1R, k1, m1L, k6) twice (56 sts).
Rnds 24–25: K.
Rnd 26: K38, (m1R, k3, m1L, k6) twice (60 sts).
Rnd 27: K.
Rnd 28: K38, (m1R, k5, m1L, k6) twice (64 sts).
Rnds 29–31: K.
Rnd 32: Cast off 2 sts, k24, cast off 4 sts, k28, cast off last 2 sts (56 sts). Slip 28 sts from chest on to first st-holder and 28 sts from back on to second st-holder. Sew gap between legs.
STUFFING STAGE 1
See page 21.

RIGHT ARM
HAND
With 2 dpns, cast on 3 sts.
Next row: Kfb into each st (6 sts). Slip 2 sts on to each of 3 dpns. Place a marker at beg of rnd.
Rnd 1: K.
Rnd 2: (Kfb, k2) twice (8 sts).
Rnd 3: K.
Rnd 4: (Kfb, k3) twice (10 sts).
Rnd 5: K.
Rnd 6: (Kfb, k4) twice (12 sts).
Rnd 7: K.
Rnd 8: (Kfb, k5) twice (14 sts).
Rnds 9–10: K.
Rnd 11: (K2tog, k5) twice (12 sts).

Rnd 12: K.
Rnd 13: (K2 tog, k4) twice (10 sts).
WRIST AND FOREARM
Rnds 14–18: K.
Rnd 19: (Kfb, k4) twice (12 sts).
Rnds 20–24: K.
Rnd 25: (Kfb, k5) twice (14 sts).
Rnds 26–30: K.
Rnd 31: (Kfb, k6) twice (16 sts).
Rnds 32–36: K.
Rnd 37: (K2tog, k6) twice (14 sts).
Rnd 38: K.
Rnd 39: (K2tog, k5) twice (12 sts).
Rnds 40–43: K.
BICEPS
Rnd 44: (Kfb, k5) twice (14 sts).
Rnds 45–46: K.
Rnd 47: (Kfb, k6) twice (16 sts).
Rnd 48: K.
Rnd 49: Kfb, k8, kfb, k6 (18 sts).
Rnd 50: K.
Rnd 51: Kfb, k10, kfb, k6 (20 sts).
Rnd 52: K.
Rnd 53: Kfb, k12, kfb, k6 (22 sts).
Rnd 54: K.
Rnd 55: Kfb, k14, kfb, k6 (24 sts).
Rnd 56: K.**
Rnd 57: Cast off 2 sts, k to last 2 sts, cast off 1 st. Cut yarn, thread through loop. Secure yarn. Beg at gap of cast-off sts, slip 10 sts on to first st-holder and 10 sts on to second st-holder. Cast-off sts form the armpit.

LEFT ARM
Work as for Right Arm to **.
Rnd 57: K16, cast off 4 sts, k4 (20 sts).
Beg at gap of cast-off sts, slip 10 sts on to first st-holder and 10 sts on to second st-holder. Cast-off sts form the armpit.

UPPER CHEST
The arms are now joined to the torso. Stuff the arms and insert pipe cleaners after a few rounds of the upper chest have been worked (see page 21). Lay the torso flat with the chest uppermost. Place right and left arms on each side

with the armpit cast-off sts facing towards the torso.

Slip sts for arms and torso from st-holders on to 4 dpns as follows:

Needle 1: 10 sts from front of left arm and 14 sts from left chest (24 sts).

Needle 2: Rem 14 sts from right chest and 10 sts from front of right arm (24 sts).

Turn doll so back is uppermost.

Needle 3: Rem 10 sts from right arm and 14 sts from right back (24 sts).

Needle 4: Rem 14 sts from left back and rem 10 sts from left arm (24 sts). (96 sts in total)

Place a marker for beg of rnd.

Rejoin yarn to start of needle 1 (front of left arm) and cont in rnds as follows:

Rnd 1: K.

Rnd 2: (K8, k2tog, skpo, k24, k2tog, skpo, k8) twice (88 sts).

Rnd 3: K.

Rnd 4: (K7, k2tog, skpo, k22, k2tog, skpo, k7) twice (80 sts).

Rnd 5: K.

Leave sts on needles but make sure sts cannot slip off (use point protectors or similar).

Stuffing Stage 2

See page 21.

Rnd 6: (K6, k2tog, skpo, k20, k2tog, skpo, k6) twice (72 sts).

Rnd 7: K.

Rnd 8: (K5, k2tog, skpo, k18, k2tog, skpo, k5) (64 sts).

Rnd 9: K.

Rnd 10: (K4, k2tog, skpo, k16, k2tog, skpo, k4) twice (56 sts).

Rnd 11: K.

Rnd 12: (K3, k2tog, skpo, k14, k2tog, skpo, k3) twice (48 sts).

Rnd 13: K.

Rnd 14: (K2, k2tog, skpo, k12, k2tog, skpo, k2) twice (40 sts).

Rnd 15: K.

Rnd 16: (K1, k2tog, skpo, k10, k2tog, skpo, k1) twice (32 sts).

Rnd 17: K.

Rnd 18: (K2tog, skpo, k8, k2tog, skpo) twice (24 sts).

Rnd 19: K.

Rnd 20: Slip last st from needle 4 on to beg of needle 1, (skpo, k8, k2tog) twice (20 sts).

Rnd 21: K.

Rnd 22: (Skpo, k6, k2tog) twice (16 sts).

NECK AND HEAD

Rnds 1–3: K.

Rnd 4: K1, (kfb into each of next 2 sts, k2) 3 times, kfb into each of next 2 sts, k1 (24 sts).

Rnd 5: K.

Rnd 6: K2, (kfb into each of next 2 sts, k4) 3 times, kfb into each of next 2 sts, k2 (32 sts).

Rnd 7: K.

Rnd 8: K3, (kfb into each of next 2 sts, k6) 3 times, kfb into each of next 2 sts, k3 (40 sts).

Rnd 9: K.

Rnd 10: K4, (kfb into each of next 2 sts, k8) 3 times, kfb into each of next 2 sts, k4 (48 sts).

Rnds 11–13: K.

Rnd 14: K11, kfb, k to end (49 sts).

Rnd 15 (make nose): K12, kfb twice into next st, turn, p4, turn, k2tog twice, turn, p2tog, turn, k to end.

Rnd 16: K11, k2tog, k to end (48 sts).

Rnds 17–18: K.

Rnd 19: K4, (k2tog, skpo, k8) 3 times, k2tog, skpo, k4 (40 sts).

Rnd 20: K.

Rnd 21: K3, (k2tog, skpo, k6) 3 times, k2tog, skpo, k3 (32 sts).

Rnd 22: K.

Rnd 23: K2, (k2tog, skpo, k4) 3 times, k2tog, skpo, k2 (24 sts).

Rnd 24: K.

Stuff the neck and head firmly.

Rnd 25: K1, (k2tog, skpo, k2) 3 times, k2tog, skpo, k1 (16 sts).

Rnd 26: K.

Rnd 27: (K2tog, skpo) 4 times (8 sts).

Rnd 28: K.

Rnd 29: (K2tog) 4 times (4 sts).

Stuff the head.

Cut yarn, leaving a long end, thread through rem sts, pull up tightly and secure yarn end.

MAKING UP

See page 20 to add facial features, hair and other details to help personalise your doll.

KNITTING REGENCY OUTFITS

BREECHES

This breeches pattern is used for many of the gentlemen. It uses approx. 28g (1oz) of 4ply (fingering) yarn. Here are the yarns used.

MATERIALS

Option 1: 1 x 50g ball Bergère de France Coton Fifty (50% cotton/50% acrylic; 50g/153yds) in shade 22493 Coco

Option 2: 1 x 100g ball Patons 100% Cotton 4ply (fingering 100% cotton; 100g/360yds) in shade 1712 Black

Option 3: 1 x 50g ball Phildar Lambswool (51% lambswool/49% acrylic; 50g/146yds) in shade 0121 Kaki

Option 4: 1 x 100g ball DMC Petra 3 (100% cotton; 100g/306yds) in shade 5712

- Pair of 2.75mm (US 2) needles
- Pair of 3.25mm (US 3) needles

TENSION

25 sts and 38 rows = 10cm (4in) over St-st

FRONT and BACK (BOTH ALIKE)

With 2.75mm (US 2) needles, cast on 25 sts. Work 4 rows in moss-st. Change to 3.25mm (US 3) needles. Cont in St-st, at the same time inc 1 st at each end every foll 4th row until you reach 37 sts. Cont without shaping until work measures 9cm (3½in). Cast off 2 sts at beg of next 2 rows (33 sts). Dec 1 st at each end of next row (31 sts). Cont without shaping until work measures 16.5cm (6½in). Change to 2.75mm (US 2) needles and work 3 rows in (k1, p1) rib. Cast off.

MAKING UP

Press pieces lightly on WS using a warm iron over a damp cloth. Join the front and back seams, then sew the inner leg seams. Darn in ends.

TROUSERS

This pattern for trousers is used for some of the gentlemen in the book where breeches aren't required. Each pair uses approx. 28g (1oz) of 4ply (fingering) yarn. Here are the yarns used.

MATERIALS

Option 1: 1 x 50g ball Adriafil Azzurra (70% wool/30% acrylic; 50g/246yds) in shade 070 Mélange Anthracite Grey

Option 2: 1 x 50g ball Drops Alpaca Silk (70% alpaca/30% silk; 50g/183yds) in shade 8465 Medium Grey

Option 3: 1 x 100g ball Patons 100% Cotton 4ply (fingering 100% cotton; 100g/360yds) in shade 1712 Black

- Pair of 2.75mm (US 2) needles

TENSION

28 sts and 40 rows = 10cm (4in) over St-st

FRONT and BACK (BOTH ALIKE)

Cast on 35 sts. Work 4 rows in moss-st. Cont in St-st without shaping until work measures 11.5cm (4½in). Cast off 2 sts at beg of next 2 rows (31 sts). Dec 1 st at each end of next row and foll alt row once (27 sts). Cont without shaping until work measures 17.75cm (7in). Work 4 rows in (k1, p1) rib. Cast off.

MAKING UP

Press pieces lightly on WS using a warm iron over a damp cloth. Join the front and back seams, then sew the inner leg seams. Darn in ends.

GENTLEMEN'S BOOTS

This pattern for Gentlemen's Boots is used throughout the book. The boots use approx. 28g (1oz) of 4ply (fingering) yarn. Here are the yarns used.

MATERIALS

Option 1: 1 x 100g ball Patons 100% Cotton 4ply (fingering 100% cotton; 100g/360yds) in shade 1712 Black

Option 2: 1 x 50g ball Scheepjeswol Cotton 80 (100% cotton; 50g/295yds) in shade 657 Dark Brown

Option 3: 1 x 50g ball Phildar Lambswool (51% lambswool/49% acrylic; 50g/146yds) in shade 0121 Kaki

- Pair of 3.25mm (US 3) needles
- Small amount of thin cardboard
- Spray starch or fabric stiffener

MAIN BOOT

Cast on 40 sts. Work 2 rows in garter-st, then cont in St-st as follows:

Next row (RS): K15, skpo, k6, k2tog, k15 (38 sts).

Next row: P15, p2tog, p4, p2tog tbl, p15 (36 sts).

Next row: K15, skpo, k2, k2tog, k15 (34 sts).

Next row: P15, p2tog twice, p15 (32 sts).

Next row: K15, k2tog, k15 (31 sts).

Next row: P12, cast off 7 sts, p12 (24 sts).

Next row: K across all 24 sts on needle.

Cont in St-st, at the same time inc 1 st at each end 3rd and every foll 4th row to 30 sts. Work 4 rows without shaping. Work 4 rows in garter-st (every row k). Cast off.

SOLE

Cast on 3 sts.

Row 1 (RS): Kfb, k to last st, kfb (5 sts).

Row 2: K.

Row 3: Rep Row 1 (7 sts).

K 17 rows.

Next row: K2tog, k to last 2 sts, k2tog (5 sts).

Next row: K.

Next row: K2tog, k1, k2tog (3 sts). Cast off.

MAKING UP

Press all pieces lightly on WS using a warm iron over a damp cloth, applying spray starch or fabric stiffener if possible. Fold the cast-off edge of the Main Boot foot and sew together (to create the top of the boot's foot). Sew the back seam of the Main Boot. Oversew the Sole to the Main Boot, making sure the fronts and backs match. Darn in ends. Cut a small piece of cardboard the same shape as the Sole and place in the bottom of the Boot.

SHIRT

This shirt pattern is used for most of the gentlemen in the book, except for the dueling shirts on page 82. The shirt and cravat use approx. 28g (1oz) of 4ply (fingering) yarn. Here are the yarns used.

MATERIALS

Option 1: 1 x 25g ball Jamieson & Smith 2ply Weight (laceweight, 100% Shetland wool; 25g/125yds) in shade 01A Cream

Option 2: 1 x 100g ball DMC Petra 3 (100% cotton; 100g/306yds) in shade 5712

Option 3: 1 x 100g ball Patons 100% Cotton 4ply (fingering 100% cotton; 100g/360yds) in shade 1691 White

- Pair of 3.25mm (US 3) needles
- 3 stitch holders
- 3 small buttons

TENSION

28 sts and 36 rows = 10cm (4in) over St-st

BACK

Cast on 31 sts. Work 2 rows in (k1, p1) rib.* Cont in St-st until work measures 6.25cm (2½in).

Armhole

Cast off 2 sts at beg of next 2 rows (27 sts). Dec 1 st at each end of next row (25 sts). Cont without shaping until Armhole measures 5.75cm (2¼in). Cast off 8 sts, sl next 9 sts on to a st-holder, cast off 8 sts.

FRONT

Follow instructions for Back to *. Work 8 rows in St-st.

Next row (RS): K14, p1, k1, p1, turn. Cont on these 17 sts only for Left Front.

Next row: P1, k1, p to end. Cont to work in est patt for another 2.5cm (1in), working 3 sts in moss-st at the button-band edge.

Next row (buttonhole): K14, cast off 2 sts, p1.

Next row (buttonhole): P1, cast on 2 sts, p to end.

Cont in est patt, working 2 more buttonholes 2.5cm (1in) apart. At the same time, when work measures 6.25cm (2½in), ending on a WS, shape armhole.

Armhole

Next row: Cast off 2 sts, work in patt to end (15 sts).

Next row: Work in patt to end.

Next row: K2tog, work in patt to end. Work in patt without shaping until Armhole measures 4.5cm (1¾in) ending on a RS.

Next row: Moss-st 3, place those 3 sts on to a st-holder, p to end.

Next row: K9, k2tog (10 sts).

Next row: P2tog, p to end (9 sts).

Next row: K7, k2tog (8 sts). Cast off. With RS facing, rejoin yarn to rem 14 sts for the Right Front. Cast on 3 sts for button band.

Next row: P1, k1, p1, k to end.

Next row: P to last 2 sts, k1, p1. Cont to rep last 2 rows until work measures 6.25cm (2½in), ending on a RS.

Next row: Cast off 2 sts, p to end.

Next row: K.

Next row: P2tog, p to end. Cont in patt without shaping until Armhole measures 4.5cm (1¾in), ending on a WS.

Next row: Moss-st 3, place those 3 sts on to a st-holder, k2tog, k to end.

Next row: P to last 2 sts, p2tog.

Next row: K2tog, k to end. Cast off.

SLEEVES (MAKE 2)

Cast on 18 sts. Work 2 rows in (k1, p1) rib. Cont in St-st, at the same time inc 1 st at each end of every foll 4th row to 28 sts. Cont until work measures 9cm (3½in). Cast off 2 sts at beg of next 2 rows. Dec 1 st at each end of every row until 4 sts rem. Cast off.

COLLAR

Sew shoulders together. With RS facing, rejoin yarn to beg of 3 moss-sts on Right Front shoulder st-holder. P1, k1, p1, then pick up and k4 sts along right side neck, 9 sts from st-holder at Back, 4 sts from left-hand side neck, then moss-st across 3 sts on st-holder.

Work 3 rows in moss-st.

Next row (RS): K2tog, moss-st to last 2 sts, k2tog. Cast off.

CRAVAT

Cast on 7 sts. Cont in moss-st until work measures 7.5cm (3in). K2tog at each end of next row (5 sts). Cont without shaping until work measures 35cm (14in). Inc 1 st at each end of foll row. Cont without shaping until work measures 43cm (17in). Cast off.

MAKING UP

Press all pieces lightly on WS using a warm iron over a damp cloth. Sew the overlap button band so that the right button band fits under the left button band. Sew shoulder, side and sleeve seams, then sew Sleeves into armholes. Attach 3 small buttons to right front button band corresponding to buttonholes. Darn in ends.

GENTLEMEN'S WAISTCOAT

This waistcoat pattern is used for many of the gentlemen in the book,

except where stated. It uses approx. 28g (1oz) of 4ply (fingering) yarn. Here are the yarns used.

MATERIALS

Option 1: Rowan Pure Wool 4ply (fingering 100% wool; 50g/174yds) in shade 461 Ochre

Option 2: 1 x 50g ball Red Heart Miami (100% cotton; 50g/131yds) in shade 139 Grey Brown

Option 3: 1 x 100g ball DMC Petra 3 (100% cotton; 100g/306yds) in shade 54462

• Pair of 3.25mm (US 3) needles
• 3 small beads

TENSION

27 sts and 37 rows = 10cm (4in) over St-st

BACK

Cast on 33 sts. Work 2 rows in moss-st. Cont without shaping in St-st until work measures 5cm (2in), ending on a WS.

Armhole

Cast off 2 sts at beg of next 2 rows (29 sts). Dec 1 st at each end of next and foll alt row (27 sts). Cont without shaping until Armhole measures 6.25cm (2½in).

Next row (RS): Cast off 8 sts, work 9 sts in moss-st, cast off 8 sts.

Break yarn.
With RS facing, rejoin yarn to rem 9 sts. Work 5 rows in moss-st. Cast off.

LEFT FRONT

Cast on 19 sts. Work 2 rows in moss-st.
Next row (RS): K to last 2 sts, p1, k1.
Next row: K1, p1, k1, p to end.
Cont without shaping in St-st with moss-st button band until work measures 5cm (2in), ending on a WS.

Armhole
Cast off 2 sts at beg of next row (17 sts). Patt 1 row.
Next row (RS): K2tog, k to last 4 sts, (p1, k1) twice (16 sts).

Next row: K1, p1, k1, p to end.
Next row: K2tog, k to last 4 sts, (p1, k1) twice (15 sts).
Next row: (K1, p1) twice, k1, p to end.
Next row: K to last 6 sts, (p1, k1) 3 times.
Next row: (K1, p1) twice, k1, p to end.
Rep last 2 rows twice.
Next row: K to last 8 sts, (p1, k1) 4 times.
Next row: (K1, p1) 4 times, p to end. Rep last 2 rows until armhole measures 5cm (2in), ending on a WS.
Next row: Cast off 8 sts (7 sts). Cont in moss-st on rem 5 sts for 5 rows. Cast off.

RIGHT FRONT

Follow for Left Front, reversing shapings.

MAKING UP

Press all pieces lightly on WS using a warm iron over a damp cloth. Sew shoulder and continuation collar seams. Sew side seams and attach small beads to left front button band, overlapping the left front over the right slightly and securing the fronts so that they are attached. Darn in ends.

LADIES' SHOES

All the ladies wear these shoes. Here are the yarns used.

MATERIALS

- Small amount of 4ply (fingering) yarn in desired colour
- Pair of 3.25mm (US 3) needles
- Small beads or coloured/metallic thread to decorate

SOLES (MAKE 2)

Cast on 3 sts.
Row 1 (WS): K1, p1, k1.
Row 2: Kfb, p1, kfb (5 sts).
Row 3: (P1, k1) twice, p1.
Row 4: Kfb, k1, p1, k1, kfb (7 sts).
Row 5: (K1, p1) 3 times, k1.
Row 6: Kfb, (k1, p1) twice, k1, kfb (9 sts).
Row 7: P1, (K1, p1) 4 times.
Rows 8–15: As Row 7.
Row 16: K2tog, (k1, p1) twice, k1, k2tog (7 sts).
Row 17: As Row 5.
Row 18: K2tog, k1, p1, k1, k2tog (5 sts).
Row 19: As Row 3.
Row 20: K2tog, k1, k2tog (3 sts). Cast off.

UPPERS (MAKE 2)

Cast on 5 sts.
Row 1 (RS): (K1, p1) twice, k1.

Row 2: As Row 1.
Row 3: Kfb, p1, k1, p1, kfb (7 sts).
Row 4: (P1, k1) 3 times, p1.
Row 5: Kfb, (k1, p1) twice, k1, kfb (9 sts).
Row 6: (K1, p1) 4 times, k1.
Row 7: Kfb, (k1, p1) 3 times, k1, kfb (11 sts).
Row 8: Moss-st 4, turn. Cont on these 4 sts in moss-st, work 10 more rows. Cast off. With RS facing, return to rem 7 sts and rejoin yarn.
Next row (RS): Cast off 3 sts, moss-st to end. Cont on these 4 sts in moss-st, work 10 more rows. Cast off.

MAKING UP

Sew the cast-off edges of the upper. Sew the Upper to the Sole, making sure the front and back are centred correctly. Decorate and embellish as desired.

Basic techniques

There are some very specific techniques used in this book, so here's a guide to some of the more common ones featured throughout. For extra techniques, see pages 108–9.

Doll Skeletons

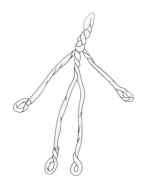

For the purposes of this book, the figures are made more flexible by creating a 'skeleton' from armature wire, which is gradually inserted into the knitting as you go along. Armature wire can be bought online from model-making websites or from some specialist hobby and art shops. You can use alternatives such as florist's wire, galvanised wire or jumbo pipe cleaners, but you can't beat armature wire for its soft but tough flexibility.

For each limb, cut a length of wire to fit the legs or arms, then loop the end to form a foot or hand and twist it back on itself to avoid sharp edges (see illustration above). Push to the end of the leg or arm to form the toes or fingers. Once you have

stuffed the appropriate section, twist the ends of each leg or arm together to give it some structure. You will effectively be forming a skeleton as you go. (The illustration on the left shows roughly how the wire will look inside the doll.)

Facial Features

For the eyes, mark the position lightly with a pencil or use pins. Using a length of 4ply (fingering) yarn and a darning needle, work a French knot (see page 108). Take the yarn to the back of the head and fasten off.

To make a lady's eyelashes, work the French knot and then bring the yarn through to the front again next to the eye and form a very small loop. Take the yarn to the back of the head and fasten off, keeping the loop loose. Cut the loop and trim, fluffing out the ends to form the eyelashes.

The mouth is sewn with red yarn using a backstitch, or cut out some red felt and sew it on with a couple of small securing stitches.

Glasses

Regency glasses were rather basic; to re-create them, twist a length of gold picture wire into the appropriate shape.

Hair

The hair is created by knotting lengths of yarn into the head using a crochet hook (similar to a

rug-making technique). Have a look at these tips for ideas.

REGENCY LADIES

Powdered wigs and elaborate hairstyles were just going out of style at the time Austen was writing her works. Hair was tied back in a chignon to show off the neck, or even worn loose at the back. Simple, unfussy ringlets and curls were teased on to the face. Ribbons tied in bands were also popular.

REGENCY GENTLEMEN

As for ladies, powdered wigs had just gone out of style at the end of the eighteenth century, and a more natural style was in favour. Hair was short, although still covering the collar at the back, and it was popular to sport artfully arranged locks on the forehead and a slightly tousled look. Curls were also combed forwards on to the forehead to resemble a Roman emperor!

HAIR INSTRUCTIONS

1. First decide roughly what sort of style you'd like for your doll – have fun watching the Austen adaptations! The best yarn to use for hair is cotton or wool (mix) 4ply, although a DK can create volume (step forward, Mr Darcy).
2. Once you've decided on the hair length, add a little extra in case of error – it's easier to cut the hair to the desired length than it is to pull it out because it's too short!
3. Cut a strip of thin cardboard to the desired length. Wrap the yarn around the cardboard until you have enough to cover the head. Cut the wrapped strands

at the bottom and remove the cardboard.

4. Decide where you want your hairline to start; you can even draw it lightly in pencil if necessary as a guide.

5. Insert a crochet hook through the knitted fabric between the stitches. Fold a strand in half and pull it through, creating a small loop. Hook the ends through the loop and pull it to tighten the knot. Experiment with where you place your hook – you'll find it will affect the direction of the hair (that is, if you want the hair to be scraped back or fall forwards).

6. Repeat over the head for the desired effect.

7. You may find that you don't need to cut the hair into shape, but instead you can sew the hair into place with a darning needle; Mr Bingley's hair, for instance, was all cut to a similar length and sewn into place at the back.

STUFFING

The figures are stuffed as you go along in the following stages:

STAGE 1
Partly stuff foot. Insert wire to end of toes. Stuff legs around wire. Stuff torso firmly. Distribute stuffing evenly and pad out the shaped sections where appropriate, ensuring there are no lumpy bits.

STAGE 2
Carefully sew up any gaps around the chest where necessary. Partly stuff the hand. Insert wire to end of fingers. Stuff arms around wire to end of fingers, evenly distributing the stuffing. Then stuff more of the torso.

STAGE 3
When you reach the neck, stuff the rest of the torso.

STAGE 4
Stuff the head when you only have five rows remaining to knit.

Don't overstuff, because this will push the knitted fabric out of shape and the stuffing will show through the knitted stitches. The shaped fabric will give you a guide as to which bits need more or less stuffing (such as calf muscles and thighs). When it comes to stuffing the limbs, make sure each one is even – it's hard to get them identical, but try to make them as similar as possible.

WRAP AND TURN (W&T)

Some of the patterns in this book use short rows, or partial knitting, as a shaping method. The work is turned before the row is completed, and worked over several rows; this creates extra fabric in one area of the knitting. When you turn the work, a hole appears when all the stitches are worked over again. Use the Wrap and Turn technique as follows to hide this hole:

Row 1 (RS): Knit to the turning point. Wrap the next st as follows: slip the st purlwise on to the right-hand needle, bring the yarn forward between the needles to RS of work. Slip the st back on to the left-hand needle, take the yarn back between the needles to WS of work, then turn the work so that the WS is facing.
Row 2: Purl the required number of sts. Wrap the next st as follows: slip the st purlwise on to the right-hand needle, take the yarn back between the needles to RS of work. Slip the

st back on to the left-hand needle, bring the yarn forward between the needles to the WS of the work, then turn the work so that the RS is facing.

Each wrapped stitch will have a strand of yarn lying across its base. When the short row section is completed and you work across all the stitches again, knit or purl the strand together with the wrapped st.

MOSS STITCH

Moss stitch is used often throughout these patterns because it makes for a firm fabric and neat edges, useful for these small items. Depending on the number of sts called for in the pattern, moss stitch is worked as follows:

Uneven number of sts
Row 1: K1, p1; rep to last st, k1. Rep for desired amount of rows.

Even number of sts
Row 1: K1, p1; rep to end.
Row 2: P1, *k1, p1; rep from * to last st, k1.
Rep these 2 rows for desired length.

PROJECTS

Netherfield Park Is Let at Last

PRIDE AND PREJUDICE

'It is a truth universally acknowledged, that a single man in possession of a good fortune, must be in want of a wife.'

Ah, the enduring appeal of the classic *Pride and Prejudice*! But for all its romance, sharp humour and tension, it is a book of its time, concerning itself with economic practicalities and social relationships.

Austen uses such warmth and charm to build her tale that these practicalities are often overlooked. In a flurry of excitement we meet Mr and Mrs Bennet at home in Longbourn House, parents to five unmarried daughters in an age when a woman's material comfort was only as good as her husband's bank account. Mrs Bennet's chief aim in life is to pair off her daughters with wealthy young men, so imagine her elation when she discovers that Netherfield, a nearby country estate, has just been let by Mr Bingley – *'A single man of large fortune; four or five thousand a year.'* She is intent on netting him and desperately tries to persuade her husband to establish contact so they can reel him in.

Mischievous Mr Bennet has every intention of paying a visit to Netherfield, but he can't resist the temptation to tease his wife, feigning a bemused indifference to the opportunity. A frustrated Mrs Bennet declares, *'You take delight in vexing me. You have no compassion for my poor nerves.'* Mr Bennet wryly counters: *'You mistake me, my dear. I have a high respect for your nerves. They are my old friends.'* When Mr Bennet eventually visits Netherfield, he does so secretly and drops the news casually in front of his wife and daughters for maximum effect – witnessing the ensuing commotion, he's not disappointed!

MRS BENNET'S DRESS

MATERIALS

- 1 x 50g ball Red Heart Baby (100% acrylic; 50g/207yds) in each of shades 8503 Pink (MC) and 8528 Cream (CC)
- Pair of 3.25mm (US 3) needles

TENSION

26 sts and 34 rows = 10cm (4in) over St-st

SKIRT AND BACK

With MC, cast on 93 sts. Work 2 rows in moss-st.

Next row (RS): K1, p1, k4, work from chart to last 2 sts, p1, k1.

Next row: K1, p1, k1, p3, work from chart to last 3 sts, k1, p1, k1.

Cont to work from chart with moss-st edges until work measures 17.75cm (7in) ending on a WS. Break CC.

Next row: K1, p1, k1, *k2 tog; rep from * to last 2 sts, p1, k1 (49 sts).

Next row: K1, p1, k1, p to last 3 sts, k1, p1, k1.

Next row: K1, p1, k2, (k2tog) 6 times, k17, (k2tog) 6 times, k2, p1, k1 (37 sts).

Next row: Cast off 9 sts, p25, k1, p1, k1 (28 sts).

Next row: Cast off 9 sts, k to end (19 sts).

Back

Cont in St-st. Work 2 rows. Inc 1 st at each end of next row (21 sts). Work 2 rows.

Armhole

Cast off 2 sts at beg of next 2 rows (17 sts). Cont without shaping until Armhole measures 4.5cm (1¾in). Cast off.

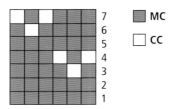

7
6
5
4
3
2
1

■ MC
□ CC

Repeat these 6 sts

BODICE

Cast on 1 st.

Next row (RS): (K1, p1, k1) into st (3 sts).

Next row: P.

Next row: Kfb, k1, kfb (5 sts).

Next row: P.

Next row: Kfb, moss-st to last st, kfb (7 sts).

Next row: Kfb, moss-st to last st, kfb (9 sts).

Cont to inc 1 st at each end every row to 19 sts. Work 2 rows. Inc 1 st at each end of next row (21 sts). Work 2 rows.

Armhole

Cast off 2 sts at beg of next 2 rows (17 sts). Work 2 rows.

Next row: K6, turn. Cont on these 6 sts.

Next row: P2tog, p to end (5 sts). Cont on these 5 sts until Armhole measures 4.5cm (1¾in). Cast off. With RS facing, rejoin yarn to rem 11 sts. Cast off 5 sts, k to end (6 sts).

Next row: P to last 2 sts, p2tog (5 sts). Cont on these 5 sts until Armhole measures 4.5cm (1¾in). Cast off.

UNDERSKIRT

With CC, cast on 43 sts. Work 2 rows in moss-st. Cont in St-st until work measures 17.75cm (7in). Cast off.

SLEEVES (MAKE 2)

With CC, cast on 30 sts. Work 6 rows in St-st.

Next row (RS): K2tog to end (15 sts). P 1 row. Change to MC. Cont in St-st, inc 1 st at each end of 4th and 8th rows (19 sts). Work 4 rows in St-st. Cast off 2 sts at beg of next 2 rows (15 sts). Dec 1 st at each end of next and every alt row until 5 sts rem. Cast off.

SCARF

With CC, cast on 10 sts. Work in (k1, p1) rib until work measures 16.5cm (6½in). Cast off.

MAKING UP

Press lightly on WS using a warm iron over a damp cloth. Sew shoulder and side seams. Sew a running st along the top of each skirt front (stopping at the side seam) and gather, ensuring a gap is left at the front for the Underskirt to peep through. Sew the Bodice points to the Skirt. Sew Sleeve seams and sew into armholes. Sew a running st along the cast-off edge of the Underskirt and gather. Fit the Underskirt to the front waistband of the Bodice, ensuring that the Skirt fronts overlap the Underskirt slightly. Sew to secure. Drape the Scarf around the neckline to give a square neck edge (see page 25) and sew to secure. Make 2 small bows in CC and sew to the centre front of the Bodice. Darn in ends.

Mr Bennet's Waistcoat

MATERIALS

- 1 x 100g ball DMC Petra 3 (100% cotton; 100g/306yds) in shade 5938
- Pair of 3.25mm (US 3) needles
- 3 small beads

TENSION

26 sts and 32 rows = 10cm (4in) over St-st

BACK

Cast on 31 sts. Work 4 rows in moss-st. Cont without shaping in St-st until work measures 6.25cm (2½in).

Armhole

Cast off 2 sts at beg of next 2 rows (27 sts). Dec 1 st at each end of next and foll alt row (23 sts). Cont without shaping until Armhole measures 6.25cm (2½in). Cast off.

RIGHT FRONT

Cast on 19 sts. Work 4 rows in moss-st.

Next row (RS): K1, p1, k to end.
Next row: P to last 3 sts, k1, p1, k1. This forms a moss-st button band at the outer edge. Cont in St-st with moss-st button band until work measures 6.25cm (2½in), ending on a RS.

Armhole

Cast off 2 sts at beg of next row (17 sts). Dec 1 st at end of next and foll alt row (15 sts). Cont without shaping until Armhole measures 6.25cm (2½in), ending on a WS.
Next row: Cast off 4 sts, k to end (11 sts).
Next row: P to last 2 sts, p2tog (10 sts).
Next row: K2tog, k to end (9 sts). Rep last 2 rows until 7 sts rem. Cast off.

LEFT FRONT

Cast on 19 sts. Work 4 rows in moss-st.

Next row: K to last 2 sts, p1, k1.
Next row: K1, p1, k1, p to end. Cont in St-st with moss-st button band until work measures 6.25cm (2½in), ending on a WS.

Armhole

Cast off 2 sts at beg of next row (17 sts). Dec 1 st at beg of next 2 alt rows (15 sts). Cont without shaping until Armhole measures 6.25cm (2½in), ending on a RS.
Next row: Cast off 4 sts, p to end (11 sts).
Next row: K to last 2 sts, k2tog (10 sts). Rep last 2 rows until 7 sts rem. Cast off.

MAKING UP

Press pieces lightly on WS using a warm iron over a damp cloth. Sew shoulder and side seams. Overlap the Left Front over the Right Front slightly and sew to secure. Sew on beads to Left Front at even intervals. Darn in ends.

Armchair

MATERIALS

- 1 x 50g ball Patons Diploma Gold 4ply (fingering 55% wool/25% acrylic/20% nylon; 50g/201yds) in each of shades 4282 Cream (A); 4200 Gold (B); 4198 Iced Green (C)
- 1 x 50g ball Scheepjeswol Cotton 8 (100% cotton; 50g/186yds) in shade 657 Dark Brown (D)
- Pair of 3.25mm (US 3) needles
- Set of 4 x 3.25mm (US 3) dpns
- Stitch marker
- 2.5cm (1in)-deep foam as follows: 12.75 x 10cm (5 x 4in) for Seat 11.5 x 10cm (4½ x 4in) for Back
- Armature wire or florist's wire
- Small amount of toy stuffing
- Small amount of thin cardboard

PATTERN NOTE: For the purposes of flexibility, the green motifs were worked in Swiss darning after the knitting was completed. The stripes were worked using two separate balls of Gold yarn (i.e., one for the set of right-hand stripes, another for the left-hand stripes) to avoid stranding at the back of the work. You may choose to work the whole pattern integrally rather than using Swiss darning, by following the chart on page 28.

SEAT

FRONT

With A and 3.25mm (US 3) needles, cast on 33 sts.
Row 1 (RS): *K3A, k2B; rep from * to last 3 sts, k3A.
Row 2: *P3A, k2B; rep from * to last 3 sts, p3A.
Rep these 2 rows until work measures 2.5cm (1in) ending on a WS.

TOP

Next row (RS): Cast on 8 sts (for side), cont to work in patt to end (41 sts).

Next row: Cast on 8 sts (for side), cont to work in patt to last 8 sts, p8A (49 sts).

Next row: K11A, *k2B, k3A; rep from * to last 8 sts, k8A.

Next row: P11A, *p2B, p3A; rep from * to last 8 sts, p8A.

Cont to rep these last 2 rows until work measures 15cm (6in). Break B, cont in A.

BACK

Next row: Cast off 8 sts, k to end (41 sts).

Next row: Cast off 8 sts, p to end (33 sts).

Cont in St-st until work measures 17.75cm (7in), ending on a RS. K 1 row.

BASE

Cont in St-st until work measures 30cm (12in). Cast off.

CHAIR BACK

BASE

With A and 3.25mm (US 3) needles, cast on 33 sts. Cont in St-st until work measures 2.5cm (1in), ending on a RS. K 1 row.

FRONT AND TOP

Next row (RS): Cast on 8 sts (for side), k11A, k2B, k3A, k2B, k13A, k2B, k3A, k2B, k3A (41 sts).

Next row: Cast on 8 sts (for side), p11A, p2B, p3B, p2B, p13A, p2B, p3A, p2B, p11A (49 sts).

Cont in patt until work measures 16.5cm (6½in), ending on a WS.

Break B, cont in A.

Next row: Cast off 8 sts, k to end (41 sts).

Next row: Cast off 8 sts, k to end (33 sts).

BACK

Cont in St-st until work measures 27.5cm (11in), ending on a RS. Cast off.

LEGS (MAKE 4)

BASE

With D and 3.25mm (US 3) dpns, cast on 1 st.

Next row (RS): (K1, p1, k1) into st (3 sts).

Next row: P.

CHAIR PATTERN CHART

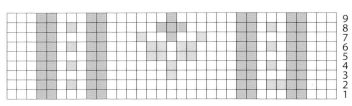

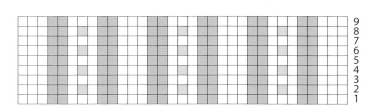

B   C

Next row: Kfb into each st (6 sts). Distribute sts evenly over 3 dpns (2 sts per dpn). Place a marker at end of rnd. Work in rnds from now on.

Next rnd: K.

Next rnd: Kfb into each st (12 sts).

LEG

Cont to k every rnd until Leg measures 6.25cm (2½in). Cast off leaving a long tail.

ARMS (MAKE 2)

With D and 2 x 3.25mm (US 3) dpns, cast on 5 sts. Work an I-cord (see page 108) measuring 25cm (10in). Cast off, leaving a long tail.

For finishing instructions see page 109.

OTHER ITEMS FROM THE SCENE

ELIZABETH'S DRESS
Follow instructions for Emma's Dress on page 62.

JANE'S DRESS
Follow instructions for Elizabeth's Dress on page 32.

BENNET'S SHIRT
See page 17. Use yarn option 2.

BENNET'S BREECHES
See page 16. Use yarn option 3.

BOOTS
See page 17. Use yarn option 1.

LADIES' SHOES
See page 19.

ELIZABETH AND MR DARCY
MEET AT MERYTON BALL

PRIDE AND PREJUDICE

'She is tolerable; but not handsome enough to tempt me'

On the surface, this is a pleasant tableau with two happy, handsome young couples, but look a little closer and you'll see that the dark-haired gentleman has a proud, standoffish look to him, and the lady with the fan is looking rather put out. This is the scene where Mr Fitzwilliam Darcy and Miss Elizabeth Bennet meet for the first time. The location is a ball at the assembly rooms in Meryton, the Bennets' nearby town. The ball is a popular occasion in the local social calendar, a chance to meet prospective suitors. Ostensibly, the focus should be on Jane Bennet and Charles Bingley, who are indeed becoming enamoured of each other and eventually make a fine couple, but the tension between Darcy and Elizabeth is too compelling to ignore.

Bingley's friend, the wealthy Darcy, makes an impressive entrance: *'The gentlemen pronounced him to be a fine figure of a man, the ladies declared he was much handsomer than Mr Bingley, and he was looked at with great admiration for about half the evening.'* Why only half the evening, you may ask? Well, it seems another side to his nature reveals itself and *'he was discovered to be proud; to be above his company, and above being pleased; and not all his large estate in Derbyshire could then save him from having a most forbidding, disagreeable countenance.'*

The final straw comes when Elizabeth overhears a conversation between Darcy and Bingley, in which Bingley is chiding him for not dancing enough. Darcy comments that Bingley is dancing with the handsomest lady in the room (Jane), but when Bingley counters that her sister Elizabeth is also attractive, Darcy replies damningly, *'She is tolerable; but not handsome enough to tempt me.'* Ouch! Elizabeth is understandably not impressed.

ELIZABETH'S DRESS

MATERIALS

- 1 x 50g ball Wendy Merino 4ply (fingering 100% wool; 50g/191yds) in shade 2365 Birch
- Pair of 3.25mm (US 3) needles

TENSION

26 sts and 34 rows = 10cm (4in) over St-st

BACK AND FRONT (BOTH ALIKE)

Cast on 48 sts. Work 3 rows in St-st. K 1 row (forms hem).

Row 1 (WS) (and all odd rows): P.
Row 2 (RS): K.

Row 4: K3, *yo, ssk, k6; rep from * to last 3 sts, k3.
Row 6: K1, *k2tog, yo, k1, yo, ssk, k3; rep from * to last 2 sts, k2.
Row 8: Rep Row 4.
Row 10: K.
Row 12: K7; rep from * of Row 4 to last st, k1.
Row 14: K5; rep from * of Row 6 to last 3 sts, k3.
Row 16: Rep Row 12.
These 16 rows form the st patt. Cont working in patt until work measures 16.25cm (6½in), ending on a Row 15.
Next row: K2tog to end (24 sts). Cont in St-st. Work 7 rows, ending on a WS.

Armhole
Cast off 2 sts at beg of next 2 rows (20 sts). Cont without shaping until Armhole measures 2.5cm (1in).
Next row: K7, turn.
**Next row: P2tog, p to end (6 sts).
Next row: K to last 2 sts, k2tog (5 sts).
Next row: P2tog, p to end (4 sts). Work 2 rows. Cast off.**
Rejoin yarn to rem 13 sts. Cast off 6

sts, then follow instructions from ** to **, reversing shaping.

SLEEVES (MAKE 2)

Cast on 18 sts. Work 2 rows in St-st.
Next row: K1, *yo, k2tog; rep from * to last st, k1.
Work 3 rows in St-st. Cast off 2 sts at beg of next 2 rows (14 sts). K2tog at each end of next and every foll alt row until 4 sts rem. Work 1 row. Cast off.

DRESS FRILL

See Mary's Dress, page 96.

MAKING UP

Press lightly on WS using a warm iron over a damp cloth. Turn under and sew picot edge on dress sides and Sleeves. Sew shoulder and side seams. Sew Sleeve seams and sew into armholes. Sew a running st around waist and neckline. Gather and secure to fit the doll. Darn in ends.

JANE'S BALL GOWN

MATERIALS

- 1 x 50g ball Phildar Relais 8 Lace (100% cotton; 50g/401yds) in Ecru
- Set of 3 x 2.75mm (US 2) dpns
- 2m x 2mm (2¼yds x 1/16in)-wide ribbon

TENSION

36 sts and 44 rows = 10cm (4in) over St-st

BACK AND FRONT (BOTH ALIKE)

Cast on 64 sts. K 1 row.
Next 3 rows: K2, *inc in next st, k5, S2KP, k5, inc in next st; rep from * to last 2 sts, k2.
Next row: K.
Row 1 (RS): K4, *(yo, ssk) twice, yo, S2KP, (yo, k2tog) twice, yo, k1, p2, k1; rep from * to last 15 sts, (yo, ssk) twice, yo, S2KP, (yo, k2tog) twice, yo, k4.

Rows 2 and 4: K3, *p13, k2; from * to last 16 sts, p13, k3.
Row 3: K3, *(yo, ssk) 3 times, k1, (k2tog, yo) 3 times, p2; rep from * to last 16 sts, (yo, ssk) 3 times, k1, (k2tog, yo) 3 times, k3. These 4 rows form trellis patt.
Rep rows 1–4.
Next 3 rows: K2, *inc in next st, k5, S2KP, k5, inc in next st; rep from * to last 2 sts, k4.
Next row: K.
Work 4 rows of trellis patt 6 times, end with Row 3. Break yarn.
Cast on 64 sts and work 4 rows of trellis patt twice, end with Row 3.
Next (joining) row: With needles parallel, WS facing and using a 3rd

needle, work Row 4 of trellis patt, working sts tog from both needles. Cont in St-st until work measures 9cm (3½in) from point of hem, ending on a RS.

**K 1 row. Work 2 rows in St-st.

Next row: K1, *yo, k2tog; rep from * to last st, k1.

Work 2 rows in St-st. K 1 row.**

Cont in St-st until work measures 14cm (5½in) from the point of hem, ending on a RS. Rep from ** to **.

Cont in St-st until work measures 19cm (7½in) from point of hem, ending on a WS.

Next row (RS): K2tog to end

(32 sts). Work 8 rows in St-st.

Armhole

Cast off 3 sts at beg of next 2 rows (26 sts). Dec 1 st at each end of next and foll alt row (22 sts). Work 8 rows in St-st. Work 2 rows in (k1, p1) rib. Cast off.

SLEEVES (MAKE 2)

Cast on 24 sts. K 1 row. Rep from ** to ** from main dress. Work 2 rows in St-st.

Next row: Kfb to end (48 sts).

Next row: P.

Cast off 3 sts at beg of next 2 rows (42 sts). Dec 1 st at each end of next

and every foll alt row until 28 sts rem, then every row until 22 sts rem. Cast off.

MAKING UP

Press very lightly on WS using a warm iron over a damp cloth. Sew shoulder and side seams. Sew Sleeve seams. Sew a running st around the top of the sleeve cap and gather tightly. Sew the bottom part of the sleeve cap into the armholes, leaving the gathered top free from the dress. Darn in ends. Thread the ribbon through the eyelet patt of the Dress and Sleeves.

DARCY'S TAILCOAT

MATERIALS

- 1 x 100g ball Patons 4ply (fingering 100% cotton; 100g/360yds) in shade 1712 Black
- Pair of 3.25mm (US 3) needles

BACK

RIGHT TAIL

**Cast on 13 sts, work 2 rows in moss-st.

Next row (RS): K1, p1, k to last 2 sts, p1, k1.

Next row: K1, p1, k1, p to last 3 sts, k1, p1, k1.

Rep last 2 rows until work measures 7.5cm (3in), ending on a WS.**

Next row (RS): K1, p1, kfb, k to last 2 sts, p1, k1 (14 sts).

Next row: K1, p1, k1, p to last 3 sts, k1, p1, k1.

Rep last 2 rows to 16 sts. Break yarn and leave 16 sts on st-holder.

LEFT TAIL

Rep from ** to **.

Next row (RS): K1, p1, k to last 3 sts, kfb, p1, k1 (14 sts).

Next row: K1, p1, k1, p to last 3 sts, k1, p1, k1.

Rep last 2 rows to 16 sts. Break yarn and leave 16 sts on st-holder.

MAIN COAT

With RS facing, rejoin yarn to 16 sts from Right tail.

Next row (RS): K1, p1, kfb, k to end, k across 16 sts from Left Tail to last 3 sts, kfb, p1, k1 (34 sts).

Next row: K1, p1, k1, p to last 3 sts, k1, p1, k1.

Rep last 2 rows, inc at each end of every RS row to 48 sts, ending on a WS.

Next row: Cast off 6 sts at beg of next 2 rows (36 sts). Cont in St-st for another 2cm (¾in).

Armhole

Cast off 2 sts at beg of next 2 rows (32 sts). K2tog at each end of next and foll alt row (28 sts). Cont without shaping until Armhole measures 5.75cm (2¼in). Cast off.

RIGHT FRONT

Cast on 26 sts.

Row 1 (RS): Moss-st 20, k6.

Row 2: P6, moss-st to end.

Row 3: K1, p1, k to end.

Row 4: P to last 3 sts, p1, k1, p1.

Rep last 2 rows 3 times more, then Row 3 once.

Armhole

Next row (WS): Cast off 2 sts, p to last 3 sts, k1, p1, k1 (24 sts).

K2tog at end of next and foll alt row (22 sts). Work 1 row.

Next row: (K1, p1) twice, k to end.

Next row: P to last 3 sts, k1, p1, k1.

Next row: (K1, p1) 3 times, k to end.

Next row: P to last 5 sts, (k1, p1) twice, k1.

Next row: (K1, p1) 4 times, k to end.

Next row: P to last 7 sts, (k1, p1) 3 times, k1.

Next row: (K1, p1) 5 times, k to end.

Next row: P to last 9 sts, (k1, p1) 4 times, k1.

Next row: (K1, p1) 6 times, k to end.

Next row: P to last 11 sts, (k1, p1) 5 times, k1.

Rep last 2 rows once.

Next row: Cast off 12 sts, k to end (10 sts).
Next row: P to last 2 sts, p2tog (9 sts).
Next row: K2tog, k to end (8 sts).
Next row: P to last 2 sts, p2tog (7 sts). Cast off.

LEFT FRONT

Rep instructions for Right Front, reversing shapings.

SLEEVES (MAKE 2)

Cast on 19 sts. Work 2 rows in moss-st. Cont in St-st, inc 1 st at each end of 4th and every foll 6th row to 31 sts. Cont without shaping until work measures 10cm (4in). Cast off 2 sts at beg of next 2 rows (27 sts). Dec 1 st at each end of next and every foll alt row until 13 sts rem. K2tog at each end of every row until 7 sts rem. Cast off.

COLLAR

Cast on 5 sts. Work in moss-st until work measures 13.5cm (5¼in).

MAKING UP

Press pieces lightly on WS using a warm iron over a damp cloth. Sew shoulder, side and sleeve seams then sew Sleeves into armholes. Sew the cast-off edges of tails on to coat Fronts. Fold back the lapels and secure with a couple of stitches. Pin the Collar on to the coat so that the centre Collar matches the centre Back, and the edges of the Collar reach the lapel. Sew to secure. Darn in ends.

FAN

MATERIALS

- 1 x 50g ball Phildar Relais 8 Lace (100% cotton; 50g/401yds) in Ecru
- Pair of 2.75mm (US 2) needles
- Small amount of 4ply (fingering) metallic gold yarn
- 5 cocktail sticks
- 5 small pearl beads

Cast on 10 sts. K 1 row.
Next row: K1, kfb; rep to end (15 sts).
K 3 rows.
Next row: K2, yo; rep to last 3 sts, k3 (21 sts).
K 3 rows.
Next row: K2, *kfb, k1, yo, k2tog; rep from * to last 3 sts, kfb, k2 (26 sts).
Next row: K4, *p3, k2; rep from * to last 7 sts, p3, k4.
Next row: K.
Next row: K4, *p3, k2; rep from * to last 7 sts, p3, k4.
Next row: K3, *kfb, k1, yo, k2tog, kfb; rep from * to last 3 sts, k3 (34 sts).
Next row: K4, *p5, k2; rep from * to last 2 sts, k2.
Next row: K.
Next row: K4, *p5, k2; rep from * to last 2 sts, k2.
Next row: K3, *kfb, k2, yo, k2tog, k1, kfb; rep from * to last 3 sts, k3 (42 sts).
Next row: K5, *p5, k4; rep to last st, k1.
Next row: K.
Next row: K5, *p5, k4; rep to last st, k1.
Next row: K5, *kfb, k2, yo, k2tog, k1, kfb, k2; rep to last 2 sts, k2 (50 sts).
Next row: K5, *p5; k6; rep from * to end.
Next row: K.
Cast off.

MAKING UP

Press very lightly on WS using a warm iron over a damp cloth. Cut down 5 cocktail sticks so that they measure approx. 5.75cm (2¼in). Using the pointed end, weave the cocktail sticks vertically and evenly in and out of the WS of the fan in between the eyelet panels, so that they form a point at the base. Splay the sticks out evenly so that the fan is spread out. Using the gold yarn, tie a knot around the base of one of the cocktail sticks and weave the yarn in and out to secure the cocktail-stick fan base. Make a small tassel out of gold yarn and sew to the bottom of the fan to cover the woven base. Darn in ends. Place one small bead at the pointed end of each cocktail stick to finish.

EVENING BAG

MATERIALS

- 1 x 50g ball Phildar Relais 8 Lace (100% cotton; 50g/401yds) in Ecru
- Pair of 2.75mm (US 2) needles
- Small amount of 4ply (fingering) metallic gold yarn

Cast on 31 sts. Work 4 rows in garter-st, then proceed in patt as follows:

Rows 1–4: K.
Row 5 (RS): *K1, (yo, k1) twice, (double yo) 5 times, (k1, yo) twice; rep from * to last st, k1.
Row 6: *K5, wyif sl 5 p'wise (dropping extra yo), k4; rep from * to last st, k1.
Row 7: *K5, wyib sl 5 p'wise, k4; rep from * to last st, k1.
Row 8: *P5, p5tog, p4; rep from * to last st, k1.
These 8 rows form the st patt. Work these 8 rows 3 more times, then Rows 1–4 once.
Next row (RS): K1, *yo, k2tog; rep from * to last 2 sts, k2.
K 3 rows. Cast off.

MAKING UP

Press very lightly on WS using a warm iron over a damp cloth. Sew the side seams, then sew the bottom seam so that the side seam is at the back of the work. Cut 4 lengths of gold yarn, each approx. 25cm (10in), thread through a darning needle and weave in and out of the eyelet pattern at the top of the bag. Finish off with a small gold tassel at one side. Cut 4 more lengths of gold yarn and make a small handle by securing at either side of the bag. Finish off with a gold tassel at the opposite side to the one already made. Darn in ends.

CHANDELIER

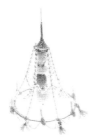

MATERIALS

- 1 x 50g ball Bergere de France Coton Fifty (50% cotton/50% acrylic; 50g/153yds) in shade 22493 Coco (MC)
- 1 x 25g ball Anchor Artiste Metallic (80% viscose/20% polyester; 25g/109yds) in shade 300 Gold (CC)
- Pair of 3.25mm (US 3) dpns
- Pair of 3.25mm (US 3) needles
- Armature wire or florist's wire
- Small amount of toy stuffing
- White pipe cleaners
- Crystal beads with centres large enough to thread gold yarn

With CC, cast on 1 st.
Row 1: (K1, p1, k1) into st (3 sts).
Row 2: K.
Row 3: P.
Row 4: Kfb to end (6 sts).
Distribute sts evenly over 3 dpns (2 sts per dpn) and cont to work in the rnd.
Next rnd: K. Change to MC.
Next rnd: Kfb to end (12 sts).
Next rnd: K.
Next rnd: K1, kfb; rep to end (18 sts).
Next rnd: K.
Next rnd: K2, kfb; rep to end (24 sts).
K 3 rnds.
Next rnd: K2, k2tog; rep to end (18 sts).
Next rnd: K.
Next rnd: K1, k2tog; rep to end (12 sts).
Next rnd: K.
Next rnd: K2tog; rep to end (6 sts). Stuff firmly.
Next rnd: K. Change to CC.
Next rnd: K1, kfb; rep to end (9 sts).
Next rnd: K.

Next rnd: K2, kfb; rep to end (12 sts).
K 2 rnds.
Next rnd: K3, kfb; rep to end (15 sts).
K 2 rnds.
Next rnd: K4, kfb; rep to end (18 sts).
K 2 rnds.
Next rnd: K4, k2tog; rep to end (15 sts).
K 2 rnds.
Next rnd: (K2tog) twice, (k3tog) 3 times, k2tog (6 sts). Stuff firmly. Change to MC.
Next rnd: Kfb to end (12 sts).
Next rnd: Kfb to end (24 sts).
K 2 rnds.
Next rnd: K2tog to end (12 sts).
Next rnd: K2tog to end (6 sts). Stuff firmly.
Next rnd: Kfb MC, k1CC; rep to end (9 sts).
Next rnd: K2MC, k1CC; rep to end.
Next rnd: KfbMC, k1MC, k1CC; rep to end (12 sts).
Next rnd: K3MC, k1CC; rep to end.
Rep last rnd twice.

Next rnd: Kfb MC, k2MC, k1CC; rep to end (15 sts).
Next rnd: K4MC, k1CC; rep to end. Rep last rnd once.
Next rnd: KfbMC, k3MC, k1CC; rep to end (18 sts).
Next rnd: KfbMC, k4MC, k1CC; rep to end (21 sts).
Next rnd: KfbMC, k5MC, k1CC; rep to end (24 sts). Break MC.
Next rnd: K.
Next rnd: K2tog, k2; rep to end (18 sts).
Next rnd: K.
Next rnd: K2tog, k1; rep to end (12 sts).
Next rnd: K.
Next rnd: K2tog to end (6 sts).
Next rnd: K2tog to end (3 sts).
Transfer sts to one dpn and create an I-cord for desired length to hang chandelier (see page 108). Cast off.

MAKING UP
Darn in Chandelier ends. Cut one piece of wire approx. 35cm (14in) in length. With CC, wrap the yarn around the wire until it is completely covered, then shape into a circle. Wrap yarn several times over the point where the circle joins and darn in end to secure.
Cut another piece of wire approx. 7.5cm (3in) in length and repeat the procedure.
Using a strand of CC, thread through crystal beads to make a beaded thread measuring approx. 12.75cm (5in), ensuring you leave long ends to attach to the wire circles – these will form the main vertical struts of the chandelier. Make 5 more the same. Divide the circumference of each gold wire circle into 6 and place markers at each point. Attach one end of the beaded threads to the markers in the small circle, then attach the other ends to the markers in the large circle.
Using a strand of CC, make another beaded thread with crystal beads measuring approx. 23cm (9in), leaving a long end of thread. Attach the end approx. halfway along one of the original 12.75cm (5in) beaded strands. You will be forming a horizontal looped circle around the main vertical struts, attaching the 23cm (9in) beaded thread to each main strut at even points all the way around (see page 31).
To make the candles, cut 6 pieces of pipe cleaner measuring approx. 2.5cm (1in). Wrap the base of the pipe cleaner with CC several times to form a 'holder'. Using CC, attach the candles at regular intervals to the large bottom gold circle. Fray out the tops of the pipe cleaners. Using a strand of CC, make another beaded thread with crystal beads measuring approx. 45cm (18in). Loop it around the bottom of the large circle, attaching it as you go. With CC, make 6 small tassels and attach them to the bottom of the large circle at regular intervals, halfway between each candle. With CC, oversew the top of the chandelier's main frame to the top of the knitted piece, so that it sits neatly over the top of the column.

OTHER ITEMS FROM THE SCENE

BINGLEY'S TAILCOAT
1 x 100g ball Drops Alpaca Silk (70% alpaca/30% silk; 50g/183yds) in shade 8465 Medium Grey Follow instructions for Darcy's Tailcoat on page 33.

BINGLEY'S WAISTCOAT
See page 18. Use yarn option 3.

BINGLEY'S TROUSERS
See page 16. Use yarn option 2.

BINGLEY'S SHIRT
See page 17. Use yarn option 1.

BINGLEY'S BOOTS
See page 17. Use yarn option 2.

DARCY'S WAISTCOAT
Follow instructions for Edmund's Waistcoat on page 98.

DARCY'S SHIRT
See page 17. Use yarn option 1.

DARCY'S BREECHES
See page 16. Use yarn option 2.

DARCY'S BOOTS
See 17. Use yarn option 1.

LADIES' SHOES
See page 19.

Lydia and Mr Wickham Are Married

PRIDE AND PREJUDICE

'My youngest sister has left all her friends – has eloped – has thrown herself into the power of – of Mr Wickham.'

This wedding comes with a tangled back story. The bride seems delighted, but notice Mr Darcy making sure the groom stays put at the altar. Though the Vicar of St Clement's seems blissfully unaware of the circumstances leading up to the event, we know better. The bride is none other than flirtatious sixteen-year-old Lydia Bennet, Elizabeth's younger sister, who went to Brighton with Mrs Forster and her husband, Colonel Forster. Unbeknownst to the Bennets, Colonel Forster happened to be in charge of a military regiment that counted a certain Mr Wickham as one of its members.

And this is none other than the groom! Much has happened since those early days when Wickham convinced Lizzy that Darcy had denied him his inheritance. When Darcy later revealed that it was Wickham who squandered his legacy, the final straw was discovering that the gold-digging Wickham had tried to elope with Darcy's fifteen-year-old sister, Georgiana, and would have succeeded, had Darcy not intervened. Just as Elizabeth is finally warming to Darcy, a bombshell is dropped . . . Lydia and Wickham have run away together – a scandal! Darcy comes to the rescue; he tracks down the wayward couple, arranges the wedding and ensures they will be financially comfortable. Mrs Bennet, inevitably, is delighted that her daughter is married. The final word, however, is given to Elizabeth: '*[H]ow little of permanent happiness could belong to a couple who were only brought together because their passions were stronger than their virtue.*'

LYDIA'S CAPE

MATERIALS

- 1 x 50g ball Red Heart Margareta (100% acrylic; 50g/257m) in shade 1109 Deer
- Small amount of cream 4ply (fingering; optional)
- Pair of 3.25mm (US 3) needles
- Stitch holder
- 3.25mm (3.25mm (D/3)) crochet hook   (optional)
- 45cm (18in) cream ribbon

TENSION

28 sts and 36 rows = 10cm (4in) over St-st

Cast on 70 sts. Work 2 rows in garter-st.

Row 1 (RS): K.

Rows 2 and 4: K2, p to last 2 sts, k1.

Row 3: K2, *(p2tog) twice, (yo, k1) 3 times, yo, (p2tog) twice; rep from * to last 2 sts, k2.

These 4 rows form the st patt. Cont in patt until work measures 17.75cm (7in), ending on a Row 4.

Next row: K2tog to end (35 sts). P 1 row.

Next row: Kfb to end (70 sts).

HOOD

Next row (WS): P35, turn. Place rem 35 sts on to st-holder.

Next row: K.

Next row: K2, p to end.

Next row (inc row): Kfb, k to end (36 sts).

Cont in St-st, working 2 sts of garter-st at hood outer edge, at the same time inc 1 st at inner seam edge on every foll 4th row to 40 sts. Cont without shaping until hood measures 8.5cm (3¼in), ending on a WS.

Next row (dec row): K2tog, k to end. Rep this dec row on foll 4th, 7th and 9th rows (36 sts), then every row until 30 sts rem. Keep sts live on needle if choosing grafting join (see page 108). If not, cast off. With RS facing, rejoin yarn to rem 35 sts and rep instructions for first part of Hood, reversing shapings.

MAKING UP

Press very lightly on WS using a warm iron over a damp cloth. Join the top of the hood seam using grafting st (see pages 108), or alternatively sew cast-off edges together. Sew back of hood. Darn in ends.

Optional Shell Neck Edging: With cream yarn and 3.25mm (3.25mm (D/3)) crochet hook, starting at bottom of Hood, join the yarn to the hood. *Make 5 tr into 1 edge st, then a little further along make a sl st into the edge; rep from * to end, working evenly as you go. Thread ribbon around neck edge and gather slightly.

WICKHAM'S MILITARY JACKET

MATERIALS

- 1 x 50g ball Scheepjeswol Cotton 8 (100% cotton; 50g/185yds in each of shades 510 Red (A), 722 Ochre (B), 502 White (C) and 515 Black (D)

- Pair of 3.25mm (US 3) needles
- 12 small gold beads
- 2 stitch holders

TENSION

28 sts and 36 rows = 10cm (4in) over St-st

BACK

TAILS (MAKE 2)

With C, cast on 1 st.

Row 1 (RS): (K1, p1, k1) into st (3 sts).

Row 2: K1, p1, k1.

Row 3: KfbC, k1A, kfbC (5 sts).

Row 4: K1C, p1C, p1A, p1C, k1C.

Row 5: KfbC, k3A, kfbC (7 sts).

Row 6: K1C, p1C, p3A, p1C, k1C.

Row 7: K1C, p1C, k3A, p1C, k1A.

Row 8: Rep Row 6.

Row 9: KfbC, k5A, kfbC (9 sts).

Row 10: K1C, p1C, p5A, p1C, k1C.

Row 11: K1C, p1C, k5, p1C, k1C.

Rows 12–13: Rep Rows 10–11.

Row 14: Rep Row 10.

Row 15: KfbC, k7A, kfbC (11 sts).

Row 16: K1C, p1C, p7A, p1C, k1C.

Row 17: K1C, p1C, k7, p1C, k1C.

Row 18: Rep Row 16.

Row 19: KfbC, k9A, p1C, k1C (13 sts).

Row 20: K1C, p1C, p9A, p1C, k1C.

Row 21: K1C, p1C, k9A, p1C, k1C.

Row 22: Rep Row 20.

Cont to work in this way (increasing 1 st at each end of every 4th row, maintaining a 2-st moss-st edge in C), until you reach 23 sts. Place sts on to st-holder.

Next row (RS): With RS facing, rejoin A yarn and work across both tails as follows: K1C, p1C, k19A, p1C, k1C, k19A, k1C, p1C (46 sts).

Next row: K1C, p1C, p19A, p1C, k2C, p1C, p19A, p1C, k1C.

Next row: K1C, p1C, k42A, p1C, k1C. Break C.

Next row: Cast off 6 sts, k to end (40 sts).

Next row: Cast off 6 sts, p to end (34 sts).

Work 6 rows in St-st in A.

Armhole

Cast off 2 sts at beg of next 2 rows (30 sts). Dec 1 st at each end of next row (28 sts). Cont without shaping until Armhole measures 6.25cm (2½in). Cast off.

RIGHT FRONT

With B, cast on 17 sts. Work 2 rows in moss-st.

Row 3: K1B, p1B, moss-st in C to end.

Row 4: Moss-st in C to last 2 sts, p1B, k1B.

Row 5: Rep Row 3.

Row 6: Cast on 6 sts in A, p to last 2 sts, p1B, k1B (23 sts).

Row 7: K1B, p1B, k in A to end. Rep Rows 6–7 three more times.

Armhole

Next row: Cast off 2 sts, p in A to last 2 sts, p1B, k1B (21 sts).

Next row: K1B, p1B, k in A to last 2 sts, k2tog (20 sts).

Next row: P in A to last 2 sts, p1B, k1B.

Next row: K1B, p1B, k1D, k in A to end.

Next row: P in A to last 4 sts, p1D, k1D, p1B, k1B.

Next row: K1B, p1B, k1D, p1D, k1D, k in A to end.

Next row: P in A to last 6 sts, (p1D, k1D) twice, p1B, k1B.

Next row: K1B, p1B, k1D, p1D) twice, k1D, k to end in A.

Next row: P in A to last 8 sts, (p1D, k1D) 3 times, p1B, k1B.

Next row: K1B, p1B, (k1D, p1D) 3 times, k1D, k to end in A.

NB: In order to avoid yarn colour changes appearing on the opposite side of the lapel (which will be folded back), from this point on start twisting your yarns at the front of the work when you change colour from A to D.

Next row: P in A to last 10 sts, (p1D, k1D) 4 times, p1B, k1B.

Next row: K1B, p1B, (k1D, p1D) 4 times, k to end in A.

Next row: P in A to last 10 sts, (p1D, k1D) 4 times, p1B, k1B.

Next row: K1B, p1B, (k1D, p1D) 4 times, k to end in A.

Next row: P10A, p8D, p1B, k1B. Break D.

Next row: K1B, p1B, k8B, k to end in A.

Next row: P10A, moss-st 10B.

Next row: Cast off 10 sts in B, k to end in A (10 sts). Break B.

Next row: P to last 2 sts, p2tog (9 sts).

Next row: K2tog, k to end (8 sts).

Next row: P to last 2 sts, p2tog (7 sts). Cast off.

SLEEVES (MAKE 2)

With D, cast on 21 sts. Work 8 sts in moss-st. Break D. Work 2 rows in St-st in C. Break C. Cont in A in St-st, at the same time inc 1 st at each end of every 8th row to 29 sts. Cont without shaping until work measures 10cm (4in), ending on a WS. Cast off 2 sts at beg of next 2 rows. Dec 1 st at each end of next and foll alt rows until 11 sts rem. Dec 1 st at each end of every row until 7 sts rem. Cast off.

COLLAR

With B, cast on 39 sts. Moss-st 1 row.

Next row (WS): K1B, p1B, p to last 2 sts in A, p1B, k1B.

Next row: K1B, p1B, skpoA, k to last 4 sts in A, k2togA, p1B, k1B (37 sts). Break A, cont in B.

Next row: K1, p1, p2tog, p to last 4 sts, p2tog, p1, k1 (38 sts). Work 1 row in moss-st. Cast off.

EPAULETTES (MAKE 2)

With B, cast on 11 sts. Moss-st 1 row.

Next row: K1B, p1B, p7A, p1B, k1B.

Next row: K1B, p 1B, skpoA, k3A, k2togA, p1B, k1B (9 sts).

Next row: K1B, p1B, p2togA, k1B, p2togA, p1B, k1B (7 sts).

Next row: K1B, p1B, k3togA, p1B, k1B (5 sts). Break A.

Next row: P2tog, p1, p2tog (3 sts). Cast off.

SHOULDER STRAPS (MAKE 2)

With B, cast on 3 sts. Work 10 rows in moss-st. Cast off.

CRAVAT

Follow instructions for Cravat for Shirt on page 18 using yarn 4.

MAKING UP

Press pieces lightly on WS using a warm iron over a damp cloth. Sew shoulder, side and sleeve seams, then sew Sleeves into armholes. Sew the cast-off edges of tails on to coat Fronts, matching up the white and gold edgings. Fold back the lapels and secure with a couple of stitches. Pin the Collar on to the coat so that the centre Collar matches the centre Back, and the edges of the Collar reach the lapel. Sew to secure. Sew Epaulettes to top of Sleeves. Sew Shoulder Straps along top of shoulders. Sew small gold beads to the front of the jacket for buttons, then 1 each on to the end of the Shoulder Straps, 1 each on to the lapels and 1 on to each cuff (see picture). Darn in ends.

VICAR'S TUNIC

MATERIALS
- 1 x 50g ball Scheepjeswol Cotton 8 (100% cotton; 50g/185yds) in shade 502 Black
- Pair of 4mm (US 6) needles

TENSION
24 sts and 32 rows = 10cm (4in) over St-st

BACK AND FRONT (BOTH ALIKE)
Cast on 35 sts, work 4 rows in moss-st. Cont in St-st, at the same time dec 1 st at each end of every 12th row until 29 sts rem. Cont without shaping until work measures 15cm (6in).

Armhole
Cast off 2 sts at beg of next 2 rows (25 sts). Dec 1 st at each end of foll row (23 sts). Cont without shaping until Armhole measures 5.75cm (2¼in), ending on a WS.
Next row: K8, turn. Cont on these 8 sts for left shoulder.

Next row: P2tog, p to end (7 sts).
Next row: K to last 2 sts, k2tog (6 sts).
Next row: P2tog, p to end (5 sts). Cast off. Break yarn.
With RS facing, rejoin yarn to rem 15 sts. Cast off 7 sts, k to end (8 sts).
Next row: P to last 2 sts, p2tog (7 sts).
Next row: K2tog, k to end (6 sts).
Next row: P to last 2 sts, p2tog (5 sts).
Cast off.

MAKING UP
Press pieces lightly on WS using a warm iron over a damp cloth. Join the shoulder seams. Join the short side seams.

DARCY'S COAT

MATERIALS
- 1 x 50g ball Regia 4ply (fingering 75% wool/25% nylon; 50g/229yds) in shade 2740 Indigo
- Small amount of black 4ply yarn for Collar
- Pair of 3.25mm (US 3) needles

TENSION
27 sts and 34 rows = 10cm (4in) over St-st

Follow instructions for Willoughby's Riding Coat on page 77, working the collar in black 4ply (fingering) yarn.

OTHER ITEMS FROM THE SCENE

LYDIA'S DRESS
Follow instructions for Elizabeth's dress on page 32, omitting Dress Frill.

WICKHAM'S MILITARY BREECHES
See page 16. Use yarn option 1.

WICKHAM'S BOOTS
See page 17. Use yarn option 1.

DARCY'S BREECHES
See page 16. Use yarn option 2.

DARCY'S SHIRT
See page 17. Use yarn option 1.

DARCY'S WAISTCOAT
See page 18. Use yarn option 2.

DARCY'S AND VICAR'S BOOTS
See page 17 Use yarn options 2 and 3, respectively.

LYDIA'S SHOES
See page 19.

VICAR'S SURPLICE
Follow instructions for Vicar's Surplice on page 68.

BIBLE
Follow instructions on page 69.

Darcy Proposes to Elizabeth (Again)

PRIDE AND PREJUDICE

'My affections and wishes are unchanged; but one word from you will silence me on this subject forever.'

Here it is, the moment we've all been waiting for. Mr Darcy proposes to Elizabeth, who graciously accepts . . . but what a roller coaster of emotions these two have ridden since first meeting at the Meryton Ball. For this certainly isn't the first time Darcy has declared his love for our Lizzy. Remember his first disastrous attempt? Elizabeth had just found out that he was responsible for separating her beloved sister Jane and his dear friend Bingley, believing Jane to be inferior in class and indifferent. He blurted out, *'You must allow me to tell you how ardently I admire and love you.'* Astonished and resentful, Elizabeth listed every reason why she disliked him.

We gain hints along the way that Darcy finds it increasingly hard to resist his attraction to Elizabeth, but her change of heart begins after his first proposal, when she discovers the truth about Mr Wickham. Her feelings are given a boost by the part he plays in Lydia and Wickham's marriage. They are cemented by her visit to Darcy's ancestral home, and we hear, *'[S]he felt that to be mistress of Pemberley might be something!'* – funny how persuasive a large country estate can be! Later, when sister Jane asks how long she's loved Darcy, Elizabeth replies: *'It has been coming on so gradually, that I hardly know when it began. But I believe I must date it from my first seeing his beautiful grounds at Pemberley.'* Another wry recognition from Austen of how wealth can give love a little nudge.

The proposal is suitably understated, but we have no doubt about Darcy's reaction. So forgive a little fantasy of what might have been had they given vent to their feelings, as we picture Darcy raising Elizabeth in the air in joy!

Elizabeth's Dress

MATERIALS

- 1 x 100g ball DMC Petra 3 (100% cotton; 100g/306yds) in each of shades 5145 Pale Blue (MC) and Ecru (CC)
- Pair of 3.25mm (US 3) needles
- Pair of 2.75mm (US 2) needles
- 3.25mm (D/3) crochet hook (optional)

TENSION

28 sts and 36 rows = 10cm (4in) over St-st

SKIRT BACK AND FRONT
(BOTH ALIKE)

With CC, and 3.25mm (US 3) needles, cast on 67 sts.
Row 1: K1, yo, *k5, sl the 2nd, 3rd, 4th and 5th sts over first st, yo, rep from * to last st, k1.
Row 2: P1, *(p1, yo, k1 tbl) into yo, p1; rep from * to end (57 sts).
Row 3: K2, k1 tbl, *k3, k1 tbl; rep from * to last 2 sts, k2.
Row 4: K.
Change to MC and cont without shaping in St-st until work measures 18.5cm (7¼in).
Next row: K1, (k2tog) 10 times, k20, (k2tog) to end (41 sts).
Change to 2.75mm (US 2) needles, work 3 rows in (k1, p1) rib. Cast off.

BODICE BACK

With MC and 3.25mm (US 3) needles, cast on 22 sts. *Work 4 rows in St-st.
Armhole
Cast off 2 sts at beg of next 2 rows (18 sts). K2tog at each end of foll row (16 sts). Work 4 rows in St-st.
Right shoulder
Next row: K7, turn. Work on these 7 sts.
Next row: P2tog, p to end (6 sts).
Next row: K.
Rep last 2 rows twice (4 sts). P1 row. Cast off.*
With RS facing, rejoin yarn to rem 9 sts. Cast off 4 sts. Rep shaping for Right shoulder, reversing shaping. Cast off.

BODICE FRONT

With MC and 3.25mm (US 3) needles, cast on 30 sts. Rep instructions for Bodice back from * to *. With RS facing, rejoin yarn to rem 17 sts. Cast off 10 sts. Rep shaping for Right Shoulder, reversing shaping. Cast off.

SLEEVES (MAKE 2)

With MC and 3.25mm (US 3) needles, cast on 30 sts. Work 4 rows in St-st. Cast off 2 sts at beg of next 2 rows. K2tog at each end of next row. Cont in St-st until work measures 5cm (2in). K2tog at each end of next 2 rows. Cast off.

MAKING UP

Press all pieces lightly on WS using a warm iron over a damp cloth. Sew Skirt edges together. Sew bodice shoulder and side seams. Sew Sleeve seams. Sew a running st along Sleeve cast-off edges and gather until they fit the armhole. Secure and sew Sleeves into Bodice. Sew a running st along lower Sleeve edge and gather to fit doll's arm. Sew a running st along Front Bodice neck edge and gather slightly to match Back Bodice neck edge. Sew Bodice to Skirt, placing Skirt seam at centre back. Darn in ends.
Optional Shell Neck Edging: With CC, starting at shoulder, join the yarn to the dress neck. *Make 5 tr into 1 edge st, then a little further along make a sl st into the edge; rep from * to end, working evenly as you go.

DARCY'S COAT

MATERIALS

- 1 x 50g ball Adriafil Azzurra (70% wool/30% acrylic; 50g/246yds) in shade 070 Mélange Anthracite Grey
- Pair of 3.25mm (US 3) needles

TENSION

28 sts and 40 rows = 10cm (4in) over St-st

BACK

Cast on 47 sts. Work 4 rows in moss-st. Cont in St-st, at the same time dec 1 st at each end of 6th and every foll 10th row to 36 sts. Cont without shaping until work measures 14.5cm (5¾in).

Armhole

Cast off 2 sts at beg of next 2 rows (32 sts). Dec 1 st at each end of foll row (30 sts). Cont without shaping until Armhole measures 7cm (2¾in). Cast off.

RIGHT FRONT

Cast on 27 sts. Work 4 rows in moss-st.

Next row (RS): P1, k1, p1, k to end.
Next row: P1, k1, p to end.
These 2 rows form the patt. Work in patt, at the same time dec 1 st at beg of 6th and every foll 10th WS row until 22 sts rem. Cont without shaping until work measures 14.5cm (5¾in), ending on a RS.

Armhole

Cast off 2 sts at beg of next row. Work 1 row. K2tog at beg of next row.
Next row: (P1, k1) twice, p1, k to end.
Next row: P to last 4 sts, (k1, p1) twice.
Rep last 2 rows once more.
Next row: (P1, k1) 3 times, p1, k to end.
Next row: P to last 6 sts, (k1, p1) 3 times.
Rep last 2 rows once more.
Next row: (P1, k1) 4 times, p1, k to end.
Next row: P to last 8 sts, moss-st to end.
Rep last 2 rows once more.
Next row: Moss-st 11, k to end.
Next row: P to last 10 sts, moss-st to end.
Rep last 2 rows until Armhole measures 5.75cm (2¼in), ending on a WS.
Next row: Cast off 11 sts, k to end (8 sts).
Work 3 rows in St-st. Cast off.

LEFT FRONT

Repeat instructions for Right Front, reversing shapings.

SLEEVES (MAKE 2)

Cast on 23 sts. Work 6 rows in moss-st, at the same time inc 1 st at each end of 6th row. Cont in St-st, at the same time inc 1 st at each end of every foll 6th row to 35 sts. Work 2 rows. Cast off 3 sts at beg of next 2 rows. Dec 1 st at each end of next and foll alt rows to 11 sts. Dec 1 st at each end of every row to 7 sts. Cast off.

COLLAR

Cast on 7 sts, cont in moss-st until work measures 13.5cm (5¼in). Cast off.

POCKETS (MAKE 2)

Cast on 9 sts. Work in St-st for 2cm (¾in). Moss-st 3 rows. Cast off.

MAKING UP

Press pieces lightly on WS using a warm iron over a damp cloth. Sew shoulder, side and sleeve seams, then sew Sleeves into armholes. Sew Pockets on to both Fronts. Fold back the lapels and secure with a couple of stitches. Pin the Collar on to the coat so that the centre Collar matches the centre Back, and the edges of the Collar reach the lapel. Sew to secure. Darn in ends.

TOPIARY ROSEBUSH

MATERIALS

- 1 x 50g ball DMC Natura Just Cotton (100% cotton; 50g/170yds) in shade N41 Siena (A)
- 1 x 50g ball Red Heart Margareta (100% acrylic, 281yds) in shade 01195 Green (B)
- 1 x 25g ball Rowan Fine Nordic Tweed (100% wool; 174yds) in shade 360 Arncliffe or small amount of 4ply (fingering) yarn for mud (C)
- Small amount of pink DK yarn
- Set of 4 x 3.25mm (US 3) dpns
- Approx. 16.5cm (6½in) x 8mm (¼in) wooden dowel
- Small amount of florist's foam
- Thin cardboard
- Toy stuffing

POT BASE

Using A and 2 x 3.25mm (US 3) dpns, cast on 1 st.
Next row: (K1, p1, k1) into st (3 sts).
Next row: P.
Next row: Kfb to end (6 sts).
Distribute sts evenly over 3 dpns (2 sts per dpn) and cont to work in the rnd.
Next rnd: P.

Next rnd: Kfb to end (12 sts).
Next rnd: K.
Next rnd: Kfb, k1; rep to end (18 sts).
Next rnd: K.
Next rnd: Kfb, k1; rep to end (27 sts).
Next rnd: K.
Next rnd: Kfb, k2; rep to end (36 sts).
Cast off.

POT SIDES

With A, cast on 36 sts and distribute evenly over 3 dpns (12 sts per dpn).
Rnd 1: K.
Rnds 2–3: P.
Rnds 4–10: K 7 rnds.
Rnd 11: K8, kfb; rep to end (40 sts).
Rnd 13: P.
Rnds 14–19: K 7 rnds.
Rnd 20: K9, kfb; rep to end (44 sts).
Rnd 21: P.
Rnds 22–28: K.
Rnds 29–31: P.
Cast off.

MUD

With C, cast on 1 st.
Row 1: (K1, p1, k1) into st (3 sts).
Row 2: P.
Row 3: Kfb to end (6 sts).
Rnd 4: P.
Row 5: Kfb to end (12 sts).
Distribute sts evenly over 3 dpns (4 sts per dpn) and cont to work in the rnd.
Rnd 6: K.
Rnd 7: Kfb, k1; rep to end (18 sts).
Rnd 8: K.
Rnd 9: Kfb, k1; rep to end (27 sts).
Rnd 10: K.
Rnd 11: Kfb, k2; rep to end (36 sts).
Rnd 12: K.
Rnd 13: Kfb, k3; rep to end (45 sts).
Rnd 14: K.
Cast off.

MAKING UP

Press and starch Mud and Pot Base lightly on WS using a warm iron over a damp cloth, taking extra care to try to make them as flat as possible. Sew the Base to the bottom of the Sides and oversew. Form the cardboard into a cylinder, slightly wider at the top than the bottom to fit the inside of the pot. Tape into shape and insert into the pail. Cut a small amount of plant oasis, approx. 7.5cm (3in) high (enough to stand firm in the bottom of the pot). Lightly pad around the outside and top with toy stuffing. Sew the Mud into the top of the Pot, approx. 1.25cm (½in) below the top. Darn in ends. With B, make a pom-pom (see page 108) approx 18cm (7in) in diameter. Push the dowel into the centre of the pom-pom, and carefully push the other end through the small hole in the Mud to the bottom of the oasis. Trim the pom-pom to form a conical shape (or alternative desired topiary shape). Take your time over this, trimming away small areas at a time to get it right, otherwise you might end up with a very small shape! To create the flowers, tie a knot in the end of a length of pink yarn, thread the yarn through the pom-pom and pull through so that the knot sits evenly on the pom-pom outer edge. Where you have threaded the yarn through, tie another knot so that it creates another flower. Trim ends.

ELIZABETH'S PARASOL

MATERIALS

- 1 x 50g ball Debbie Bliss Rialto Lace (100% wool; 50g/426yds) in each of shades 001 Ecru (A), 029 Leaf (B) and 026 Coral (C)
- Set of 4 x 2.25mm (US 1) dpns
- 6.5mm (K/10½) decorative crochet hook for handle (preferably with a ridged, large handle, e.g., Brittany Birch)
- Pipe cleaners or armature wire

With B, cast on 6 sts. K 1 row, then divide sts evenly over 3 dpns (2 sts on each needle), then proceed as follows:

Rnd 1 (RS): M1, k1; rep to end (12 sts).
Rnd 2 (and foll even rows): K.
Rnd 3: M1, k2; rep to end (18 sts).

Rnd 5: M1, k3; rep to end (24 sts).
Rnd 7: M1, k4; rep to end (30 sts).
Rnd 9: M1, k5; rep to end (36 sts).
Rnd 11: M1, k6; rep to end (42 sts). Join in A.
Rnd 13: KfbA, k6B; rep to end (48 sts).
Rnd 14: K3A, k4B, *k4A, k4B; rep from * to last st, k1A.
Rnd 15: KfbA, k3A, *k2B, k2A, kfbA, k3A; rep from * to last 4 sts, k2B, k2A (54 sts).
Rnd 16: K to end in A. Cont in A as follows:
Rnd 17: K6, m1, *k9, m1; rep from * to last 3 sts, k3 (60 sts).
Rnd 18 (and foll even rows): K.
Rnd 19: K7, m1, *k10, m1; rep from * to last 3 sts, k3 (66 sts).
Rnd 21: K7, m1, *k11, m1; rep from * to last 4 sts, k4 (72 sts).
Rnd 23: K8, m1, *k12, m1; rep from * to last 4 sts, k4 (78 sts).
Rnd 25: K7, m1, *k13, m1; rep from * to last 6 sts, k6 (84 sts).
Rnd 27: *Yo, ssk, k12; rep from * to end.
Rnd 28: K8, m1, *k14, m1; rep from * to last 6 sts, k6 (90 sts).
Rnd 29: K1, yo, ssk, *k10, k2tog, yo, k1, yo, ssk; rep from * to last 12 sts, k10, k2tog, yo (90 sts).
Rnd 30: K8, yo, *k15, yo; rep from * to last 7 sts, k7 (96 sts).
Rnd 31: *Yo, ssk, k14, yo, ssk; rep from * to end.

Rnd 32: K9, yo, *k16, yo; rep from * to last 7 sts, yo, k7 (102 sts).
Rnd 33 (and foll odd rows): K.
Rnd 34: K9, yo, *k17, yo; rep from * to last 8 sts, k8 (108 sts).
Rnd 36: K9, yo, *k18, yo; rep from * to last 9 sts, k9 (114 sts).
Rnd 38: K9, yo, *k19, yo; rep from * to last 10 sts, k10 (120 sts).
Change to B.
Rnd 39: P.
Rnd 40: K.
Rnd 41: P.
Rnd 42: P.
Cast off.

MAKING UP

Press lightly on WS using a warm iron over a damp cloth. Cut 6 pieces of large pipe cleaners or armature wire to fit the depth of the parasol. Oversew them into the inner parasol, along the lines of the eyelet patt. Cut the hook end of the crochet hook off so that the remainder measures 15cm (6in). Sew side seam. Insert handle through hole at top and oversew into place.

DARCY'S TOP HAT

MATERIALS

- 1 x 100g ball Patons 100% Cotton 4ply (fingering 100% cotton; 100g/360yds) in shade 1712 Black
- Set of 4 x 3.25mm (US 3) dpns
- Pair of 3.25mm (US 3) needles
- Small amount of thin cardboard

BRIM

With 3.25mm (US 3) dpns, cast on 30 sts and distribute evenly over 3 needles (10 sts per needle).

Row 1 (RS) (and every odd row): K.
Row 2: K2, kfb; rep to end (40 sts).
Row 4: K3, kfb; rep to end (50 sts).
Row 6: K4, kfb; rep to end (60 sts).

Row 7: P.
Row 8: K.
Row 9: P.
Cast off.

CROWN

With 3.25mm (US 3) needles, cast on 30 sts. Cont in St-st without shaping until work measures 2.5cm (1in), ending on a WS.
Next row (RS): Kfb, k9; rep to end (33 sts).
Work 3 rows. Cast off.

TOP

With 2 x 3.25mm (US 3) dpns, cast on 1 st.
Next row (RS): K1, p1, k1 into st (3 sts).
Next row: P.
Next row: Kfb to end (6 sts).
Distribute sts evenly over 3 dpns (2 sts per dpn) and cont to work in the rnd.
Next rnd: P.
Next rnd: Kfb to end (12 sts).
Next rnd: K.

Next rnd: Kfb, k1; rep to end (18 sts).
Next rnd: K.
Next rnd: Kfb, k2; rep to end (24 sts).
Next rnd: K
Next rnd: Kfb, k3; rep to end (30 sts).
Cast off.

MAKING UP

Press all pieces lightly on WS using a warm iron over a damp cloth, applying spray starch or fabric stiffener if possible. Sew the side seam of the Crown. Pin the inner Brim to the lower edge of the Crown and oversew. Pin the Top to the top edge of the Crown and oversew. Darn in ends. Cut a length of cardboard to match the size of the Crown and tape the edges together to form a cylinder. Insert cardboard into hat.

OTHER ITEMS FROM THE SCENE

DARCY'S WAISTCOAT
See page 18. Use yarn option 2.

DARCY'S SHIRT
See page 17. Use yarn option 1.

ELIZABETH'S SHOES
See page 19.

DARCY'S TROUSERS
See page 16. Use yarn option 1.

DARCY'S BOOTS
See page 17. Use yarn option 1.

EMMA PAINTS A PORTRAIT OF HARRIET

EMMA

'What an exquisite possession a good picture of her would be! I would give any money for it. I almost long to attempt her likeness myself.'

Meet Emma Woodhouse, our *'handsome, clever and rich'* twenty-one-year-old heroine who lives with her ageing father in the town of Highbury. Life has treated her well but, in the absence of travel to broaden her headstrong mind, she likes to create her own adventures. These usually involve matchmaking and a liberal dose of misplaced good intentions. Undeterred by the wisdom of family friend Mr Knightley, Emma takes on Harriet Smith as her next project. Little is known about seventeen-year-old Harriet's background, which in the early nineteenth century means she is not destined for a society match. Yet Emma vows to turn her into a gentlewoman and find her a husband.

Although Harriet is already smitten with Mr Robert Martin, Emma believes that her friend deserves better than a mere farmer. Along comes the simpering Parson of Highbury, Mr Elton. Emma convinces herself that Mr Elton could be in love with Harriet, but just needs firm guidance, and this is where the portrait comes in. Surely a painting of Harriet that emphasises her beauty will reel Mr Elton in; the reader, of course, has realised that it is the painter rather than the subject who is the actual focus of his intentions.

Mr Knightley remarks on the folly of the enterprise, wisely commenting, *'You will puff her up with such ideas of her own beauty, and of what she has a claim to, that, in a little while, nobody within her reach will be good enough for her.'* He is proved right when Mr Elton, rejected by Emma, makes another match with a wealthy lady (much to Harriet's distress). But there is a happy outcome for Harriet, and as for Emma and Mr Knightley . . . you'll have to keep reading.

HARRIET'S JACKET

MATERIALS

- 1 x 50g ball Drops Alpaca (100% alpaca; 50g/182yds) in shade 2923 Goldenrod
- Pair of 3.25mm (US 3) needles
- 2 small beads

TENSION

38 sts and 58 rows = 10cm (4in) over St-st

BACK

Cast on 23 sts. Work 2 rows in moss-st. Work 6 rows in St-st, at the same time inc 1 st at each end of 4th row (25 sts).

Armhole

Cast off 2 sts at each end of next 2 rows (21 sts). Dec 1 st at each end of next and foll alt row (17 sts). Cont without shaping until Armhole measures 5cm (2in). Cast off.

RIGHT FRONT

Cast on 13 sts. Work 2 rows in moss-st.

Next row (RS): K1, p1, k to end.

Next row: P to last 3 sts, k1, p1, k1. Rep last 2 rows 4 more times, at the same time inc 1 st at beg of 4th row (14 sts). Work 1 more RS row.

Armhole

Cast off 2 sts at beg of next row (12 sts). Dec 1 st at end of next and foll alt row (10 sts). Cont to work in St-st with moss-st button band until work measures 6.25cm (2½in), ending on a WS. Cast off 3 sts at beg of next row (7 sts). P 1 row. Dec 1 st at neck edge on next and foll alt row (5 sts). Cast off.

LEFT FRONT

Follow instructions for Right Front, reversing shapings and the button-band edge.

SLEEVES (MAKE 2)

Cast on 17 sts. Work 4 rows in moss-st. Cont to work in St-st, at the same time inc 1 st at each end of 3rd and every foll 8th row to 23 sts. Cont without shaping until work measures 7.5cm (3in), ending on a WS.

Next row (RS): Kfb to end (46 sts). Work 7 rows in St-st.

Cast off 2 sts at beg of next 2 rows (42 sts). Dec 1 st at each end of next and foll alt rows until 32 sts rem. Dec 1 st at each end of every foll row until 24 sts rem. Cast off.

COLLAR

Cast on 3 sts. Collar is worked in moss-st throughout. Inc 1 st at beg of first and third row (5 sts). Cont without shaping until work measures 11.5cm (4½in), ending on a WS row. Dec 1 st at beg of next and foll alt row (3 sts). Cast off.

MAKING UP

Press lightly on WS using a warm iron over a damp cloth. Sew shoulder seams. Sew back collar seam and sew to Back. Sew side and Sleeve seams. Sew a running st along Sleeve tops and gather tightly. Sew Sleeves into armholes. Overlap the Right Front over the Left Front slightly and sew to secure. Sew on beads to Right Front at even intervals. Darn in ends.

EMMA'S DRESS

MATERIALS

- 1 x 50g ball Red Heart Margareta (100% acrylic; 50g/281yds) in shade 0534 Claret Red
- Length of thin cream ribbon
- Pair of 3.25mm (US 3) needles

TENSION

28 sts and 34 rows = 10cm (4in) over St-st

PATTERN NOTE: Double yo = Insert right-hand needle into next st wrapping yarn around needle twice, complete knit st.

BACK AND FRONT (BOTH ALIKE)

Cast on 51 sts.

Rows 1–4: K.

Row 5 (RS): *K1, (yo, k1) twice, (double yo) 5 times, (k1, yo) twice; rep from * to last st, k1.

Row 6: *K5, wyif sl 5 p'wise (dropping extra yo), k4; rep from * to last st, k1.

Row 7: *K5, wyib sl 5 p'wise, k4; rep from * to last st, k1.

Row 8: *P5, p5tog, p4; rep from * to last st, k1.

These 8 rows form the st patt. Cont working in patt until work measures 16.5cm (6½in), ending on Row 15.
Next row: K2tog to last st, k1 (26 sts).
Cont in St-st. Work 7 rows, ending on a WS.
Armhole
Cast off 2 sts at beg of next 2 rows (22 sts). Work 1 row. K2tog at each end of foll row (20 sts). Cont without shaping until Armhole measures 2.5cm (1in).
Next row: K7, turn.
**Next row: P2tog, p to end (6 sts).

Next row: K to last 2 sts, k2tog (5 sts).
Next row: P2 tog, p to end (4 sts). Work 2 rows. Cast off.**
Rejoin yarn to rem 13 sts. Cast off 6 sts, then follow instructions from ** to **, reversing shaping.

SLEEVES (MAKE 2)

Cast on 18 sts. Work 2 rows in St-st.
Next row: K1, *yo, k2tog; rep from * to last st, k1.
Work 3 rows in St-st. Cast off 2 sts at beg of next 2 rows (14 sts). K2tog at each end of next and every foll alt

row until 4 sts rem. Work 1 row. Cast off.

MAKING UP
Press lightly on WS using a warm iron over a damp cloth. Turn under and sew picot edge on dress sides and sleeves. Sew shoulder and side seams. Sew sleeve seams and sew into armholes. Sew a running st around waist and neckline. Tie the length of ribbon around the waist and tie a bow at the back. Gather and secure to fit the doll. Darn in ends.

MR ELTON'S COAT

MATERIALS
- 1 x 100g ball Patons 100% Cotton 4ply (fingering 100% cotton; 100g/360yds) in shade 1712 Black
- Pair of 3.25mm (US 3) needles
- 3 stitch holders

TENSION
28 sts and 40 rows = 10cm (4in) over St-st

BACK
Cast on 47 sts. Work 4 rows in moss-st. Cont in St-st, at the same time dec 1 st at each end of 6th and every foll 10th row to 37 sts. Cont without shaping until work measures 14.5cm (5¾in).
Armhole
Cast off 2 sts at beg of next 2 rows (33 sts). Dec 1 st at each end of foll row (31 sts). Cont without shaping

until Armhole measures 7cm (2¾in). Place sts on a st-holder.

RIGHT FRONT
Cast on 27 sts. Work 4 rows in moss-st.
Next row (RS): P1, k1, p1, k to end.
Next row: P to last 2 sts, k1, p1.
These 2 rows form patt. Work in patt, at the same time dec 1 st at beg of 6th and every foll 10th WS row until 22 sts rem. Cont without shaping until work measures 14.5cm (5¾in), ending on a RS row.
Armhole
Cast off 2 sts at beg of next row (20 sts). Work 1 row. K2tog at beg of next row (19 sts). Work in patt without shaping until Armhole measures 4.5cm (1¾in) ending on a WS.
Next row: Moss-st 3, place those 3 sts on to a st-holder, cast off 3 sts, k to end (13 sts).
Next row: P11, p2tog (12 sts).
Next row: Cast off 3 sts, k to end (9 sts).
Next row: P7, p2tog (8 sts). Cast off.

LEFT FRONT
Repeat instructions for Right Front, reversing shaping and moss-st button band.

SLEEVES (MAKE 2)
Cast on 24 sts. Work 6 rows in moss-st, at the same time inc 1 st at each end of 6th row. Cont in St-st, at the same time inc 1 st at each end of every foll 6th row to 35 sts. Work 2 rows. Cast off 3 sts at beg of next 2 rows. Dec 1 st at each end of next and foll alt rows to 11 sts. Dec 1 st at each end of every row to 7 sts. Cast off.

COLLAR
Sew shoulders together. With RS facing, rejoin yarn to beg of 3 moss-sts on Right Front shoulder st-holder. P1, k1, p1, then pick up and k 4 sts along right side neck, 9 sts from st-holder at Back, 4 sts from left-hand side neck, then moss-st across 3 sts on st-holder from Left Front. Work 2 rows in moss-st.
Next row (RS): K2tog, moss-st to last 2 sts, k2tog. Cast off.

MAKING UP
Press pieces lightly on WS using a warm iron over a damp cloth. Sew shoulder seams. Sew side and sleeve seams, then sew Sleeves into armholes. Darn in ends.

BIRDBATH

MATERIALS

• 1 x 50g ball Drops Alpaca (100% alpaca; 50g/182yds) in shade 501 Light Grey (MC)
• Small amount of pale blue 4ply (fingering) yarn (for water) (CC)
• Pair of 3.25mm (US 3) needles
• Set of 4 x 3.25mm (US 3) dpns
• Small amount of 2cm (¾in) deep foam, cut as follows:
• 9 x 9cm (3½ x 3½in)
• 5 x 5cm (2 x 2in)
• Small amount of toy stuffing
• Small amount of thin cardboard

LARGE PLINTH STONE

With 3.25mm (US 3) needles and MC, cast on 21 sts. Work in moss-st until work measures 2cm (¾in).
Next row (RS): Cast on 5 sts (for side), moss-st 5, k to end (26 sts).
Next row: Cast on 5 sts (for side), p to last 5 sts, moss-st 5 (31 sts). Cont to work in patt (moss-st sides and St-st centre) until work measures 10.75cm (4¼in) ending on a WS.
Next row: Cast off 5 sts, moss-st to end (26 sts).
Next row: Cast off 5 sts, moss-st to end (21 sts). Cont to work in moss-st until work measures 12.75cm (5in). Cont to work in St-st until work measures 21.5cm (8½in). Cast off.

SMALL PLINTH STONE

With 3.25mm (US 3) needles and

MC, cast on 13 sts. Work in moss-st until work measures 2cm (¾in).
Next row (RS): Cast on 5 sts (for sides), moss-st 5, k to end (18 sts).
Next row: Cast on 5 sts (for sides), moss-st 5, p to last 5 sts, moss-st 5 (23 sts). Cont to work in patt (moss-st sides and St-st centre) until work measures 7cm (2¾in), ending on a WS.
Next row: Cast off 5 sts, moss-st to end (18 sts).
Next row: Cast off 5 sts, moss-st to end (13 sts). Cont to work in St-st until work measures 9cm (3½in). Cast off.

COLUMN

With 3.25mm (US 3) dpns and MC, cast on 21 sts. Distribute sts evenly over 3 dpns (7 sts per dpn).
Rnd 1: K.
Rnd 2: K1, *k2tog, k2; rep to end (16 sts).
Rnds 3–5: K 3 rnds.
Rnd 6: K1, kfb; rep to end (24 sts).
Rnd 7: K.
Rnd 8: K3, m1; rep to end (32 sts).
Rnds 9–10: K.
Rnd 11: K4, m1; rep to end (40 sts).
Rnds 12–16: K.
Rnd 17: K3, k2tog; rep to end (32 sts).
Rnds 18–20: K.
Rnd 21: K2, k2tog; rep to end (24 sts).
Rnds 22–24: K.
Rnd 25: K1, k2tog; rep to end (16 sts).
Rnds 26–28: K.
Rnd 29: K2, k2tog; rep to end (12 sts).
Rnds 30–32: K.
Rnd 33: K2, kfb; rep to end (16 sts).
Rnd 34: K.
Rnd 35: K3, kfb; rep to end (20 sts).
Rnd 36: K.
Rnd 37: K4, kfb; rep to end (24 sts).
Rnd 38: K.

Rnd 39: K5, kfb; rep to end (28 sts).
Rnd 40: K.
Rnd 41: K6, kfb; rep to end (32 sts).
Rnd 42: K.
Rnd 43: K2, m1; rep to end (48 sts).
Rnds 44–45: K.
Rnd 46: K2, kfb; rep to end (64 sts).
Rnds 47–48: K.
Rnd 49: K3, kfb; rep to end (80 sts).
Rnd 50: K.
Rnds 51–56: Work in moss-st.
Cast off.

WATER

With CC and 3.25mm (US 3) needles, cast on 10 sts.
Row 1 (and foll odd rows): K.
Row 2: K9, w&t.
Row 4: K8, w&t.
Row 6: K7, w&t.
Row 8: K6, w&t.
Row 10: K5, w&t.
Row 12: K4, w&t.
Row 14: K3, w&t.
Row 16: K2, w&t.
Row 18: K1, w&t.
Row 20: K, remembering to pick up wrapped sts.
Row 21: K.
Rep these 21 rows 5 more times.
Cast off.

MAKING UP

Press Plinth Stones and Water lightly on WS using a warm iron over a damp cloth. Fold the knitted Large Plinth Stone around the appropriate piece of foam, then pin the cast-off edge to the cast-on edge. Sew the sides to the base. Sew the cast-on edges of the sides to the front to form a box. Sew the pinned cast-on and cast-off edges together. Darn in ends. Repeat the procedure for the Small Plinth Stone, omitting the base. Place the Small Plinth Stone centred on the Large Plinth Stone and sew securely.

Firmly stuff the Column, adding extra stuffing to the curved areas and leaving a gap at the top. Place the base (cast-on edge) of the Column centred on the Small Plinth Stone and sew. Add extra stuffing to the Column if necessary once it's sewn on to the stone to compact firmly. Using the thin cardboard, cut out a circle the same size as the Water. Place on top of the birdbath opening and press down, ensuring that the moss-st rim of the birdbath is left clear of the stuffing and juts out. Using MC, stitch across the cardboard several times in a crisscross manner to keep the stuffing flat. Place the knitted Water circle on top of the cardboard, and sew around the edges to attach to the birdbath. Darn in ends.

DOVE

MATERIALS

- 1 x 50g ball Bergere de France Coton Fifty (50% cotton/50% acrylic; 50g/153yds) in shade 22493 Coco (MC)
- Small amount of yellow 2ply (laceweight) (CC)
- Small amount of black or blue 4ply (fingering) yarn
- Pair of 2.75mm (US 2) needles
- Set of 4 x 2.75mm (US 2) dpns
- Small amount of toy stuffing

HEAD

With 2.75mm (US 2) dpns, cast on 1 st.
Row 1 (RS): (K1, p1, k1) into st (3 sts).
Row 2: Kfb to end (6 sts). Distribute sts evenly over 3 dpns (2 sts per dpn) and cont to work in the rnd.
Rnd 3: K.
Rnd 4: K1, kfb; rep to end (9 sts).
Rnd 5: K.
Rnd 6: K2, kfb; rep to end (12 sts).
Rnds 7–8: K.
Rnd 9: K7, w&t.
Rnd 10: P6, w&t.
Rnd 11: K5, w&t.
Rnd 12: P4, w&t.
Rnd 13: K3, w&t.
Rnd 14: P2, w&t.
Rnd 15: K to end of Needle 2, picking up wraps.
Rnd 16: P to end of Needle 1, picking up wraps.

BODY

Rnds 17–20: K. Stuff firmly.
Rnd 21: K1, kfb; rep to end (18 sts).
Rnds 22–23: K.
Rnd 24: K2, kfb; rep to end (24 sts).
Rnds 25–28: K.
Rnd 29: K23, w&t.
Rnd 30: P6, w&t.
Rnd 31: K5, w&t.
Rnd 32: P4, w&t.
Rnd 33: K to end, picking up wraps.
Rnd 34: K.
Rnd 35: K2, k2tog; rep to end (18 sts).
Rnd 36: K.
Rnd 37: K1, k2tog; rep to end (12 sts).
Rnd 38: K.
Rnd 39: K2, k2tog twice, k to end (10 sts). Stuff firmly.
Rnd 40: K1, k2tog twice, k to end (8 sts).

TAIL

Distribute sts evenly over 2 needles (4 sts per needle). Place the needles parallel to each other and knit sts from each needle together (4 sts). Cont working in rows on 2.75mm (US 2) needles.
Next row: P1, yo; rep to last st, p1 (7 sts).
Next row (RS): K1, p1; rep to last st, k1.
Next row: P1, k1; rep to last st, p1.
Next row: K1, p1, yo; rep to last st, k1 (10 sts).
Next row: P1, k2; rep to last st, p1.
Next row: K1, p2, yo; rep to last st, k1 (13 sts).
Next row: P1, k3; rep to last st, p1.
Next row: K1, p3, yo; rep to last st,

k1 (16 sts).
Next row: P1, k4; rep to last st, p1.
Next row: K1, p4, yo; rep to last st, k1 (19 sts).
Next row: P1, k4; rep to last st, p1.
Cast off.

WINGS (MAKE 2)

Cast on 3 sts.
Row 1 (RS): K.
Row 2: Kfb to end (6 sts).
Row 3–4: K.
Row 5: *Yo, sl1 wyib, k1; rep from * to end (9 sts).
Row 6: *Yo, sl1 wyib, k2tog; rep from * to end.
Rep Row 6 ten times.
Next row (RS): K3tog, (yo, sl1 wyib, k2tog) twice (7 sts).
Next row: (Yo, sl1 wyib, k2tog) twice, k1.
Next row: (K2tog, yo) twice, sl1 wyib, k2tog (6 sts).
Next row: (Yo, sl1 wyib, k2tog) twice.
Rep last row twice.
Next row: K3tog, yo, sl1 wyib, k2tog (4 sts).
Next row: Yo, sl1 wyib, k2tog, k1.
Next row: K2tog, k2 (3 sts).
Next row: P2tog, k1 (2 sts).
Next row: P.
Next row: K2tog. Break yarn, draw end through last st.

MAKING UP

Press Wings lightly on WS using a warm iron over a damp cloth. Attach to body in desired position. With black or blue thread, make 2 French knots (see page 108) for eyes in appropriate place.

FLOWER VINE

MATERIALS

- 1 x 50g ball Red Heart Margareta (100% acrylic; 50g/281yds) in shade 01178 Dulcet (A)
- Small amount of white 4ply (fingering) yarn (B)
- Small amount of yellow 4ply (fingering) yarn (C)
- Set of 4 x 3.25mm (US 3) dpns
- Pair of 2.75mm (US 2) dpns

MAIN VINE STEM

With A, and 2 x 3.25mm (US 3) dpns, cast on 4 sts. Work I-cord (see page 108) for desired length.

SMALL LEAF

With 2 x 3.25mm (US 3) dpns and A, pick up 3 sts from the main vine stem in desired spot. Work I-cord for desired length.
Next row: Turn, p1, k1, p1.
Next row (RS): K1, m1, p1, m1, k1 (5 sts).

Next row: P2, k1, p2.
Next row: K2, m1, p1, m1, k2 (7 sts).
Next row: P3, k1, p3.**
Next row: K3, p1, k3.
Work last 2 rows 4 more times, then rep RS row once more.
Next row: K1, skpo, k1, k2tog, k1 (5 sts).
Next row: P.
Next row: K2tog, k1, k2tog (3 sts).
Next row: P3tog. Break yarn and draw through st.

LARGE LEAF

Follow instructions for Small Leaf to **, then proceed as follows:
Next row: K3, m1, p1, m1, k3 (9 sts).
Next row: P4, k1, p4.
Next row: K4, p1, k4.
Work last 2 rows 4 more times, then rep RS row once more.
Next row: K1, skpo, k3, k2tog, k1 (7 sts).
Next row: P.
Next row: K1, skpo, k1, k2tog, k1 (5 sts).
Next row: P.
Next row: K2tog, k1, k2tog (3 sts).
Next row: P3tog. Break yarn and draw through st.

FLOWER

With 2 x 3.25mm (US 3) dpns and A, pick up 3 sts from the Main Vine Stem in desired spot. Work I-cord for desired length.
Next row: Kfb to end (6 sts).
Distribute sts evenly over 3 dpns (2 sts per needle), and cont to work in the rnd.
Next rnd: K.
Next rnd: Kfb to end (12 sts).
Next rnd: K. Break A, change to B. K 4 rnds.**
Next rnd: K2tog, yo; rep to end (forms a picot edge for petals). K 2 rnds. Break B, change to C.
Next rnd: K2tog to end (6 sts).
Next rnd: P.
Next rnd: K2tog to end (3 sts).
Break yarn leaving a long end and draw yarn through last 3 sts.
Fold Flower in on itself so that the picot edge forms petals and pull yarn end through tightly to form the Flower. Secure yarn firmly in the stalk and break.

TENDRILS

With 2 x 2.75mm (US 2) dpns, pick up 3 sts from the main vine stem in desired spot. Work I-cord for desired length.

OTHER ITEMS FROM THE SCENE

HARRIET'S DRESS
Follow instructions for Anne's Dress on page 88, adding Emma's Wedding Dress Bandeau on page 68.

ELTON'S SHIRT
See page 17. Use yarn option 4.

ELTON'S TROUSERS
See page 16. Use yarn option 3.

BOOTS
See page 17. Use yarn option 1.

LADIES' SHOES
See page 19.

CAT
Follow instructions for Cat on page 98.

EMMA INSULTS MISS BATES AT THE BOX HILL PICNIC

EMMA

'I must make myself very disagreeable, or she would not have said such a thing to an old friend.'

Here's Emma Woodhouse again, still determined to play her self-appointed role as accomplice to fate and pair everybody up, but she begins to realise that she can sometimes get it disastrously wrong. This scene at the Box Hill picnic is one of those times. So who do we have at the party? There's the boorish Mr Elton and his insufferable new wife, and the disadvantaged Miss Bates and her niece Jane Fairfax. Cheerful and a relentless chatterbox, Miss Bates is unmarried and dependent upon the good wishes of her friends, while Jane Fairfax is secretly engaged to Frank Churchill. Churchill is trying to conceal his attachment to Jane by flirting outrageously with Emma. Emma is desperately trying to fix Harriet up with an eligible gentleman, but Harriet is in love with a poor farmer. Finally, we have the steady Mr Knightley and sharp-tongued Emma herself. They don't know it yet but this is a pivotal point in their relationship.

Emma is at her most mischievous in this scene, hankering after some fun and bemoaning the fact that everyone is so listless. She suggests a game in which everyone should produce either *'one thing very clever . . . or two things moderately clever; or three things very dull indeed.'* Miss Bates good-naturedly comments that she will have no trouble meeting the last requirement, to which Emma responds, *'Ah! ma'am, but there may be a difficulty. Pardon me, but you will be limited as to number – only three at once.'* Oh dear . . . even cheerful Miss Bates doesn't fail to see the meaning and a pall is cast over the already tense company as they drift apart. Mr Knightley later reprimands Emma, *'It was badly done, indeed!'* and she leaves in tears.

EMMA'S DRESS

MATERIALS

- 1 x 100g ball Rico Maxi Cotton (100% cotton; 1004mm (G/6)12yds) in each of shades Tia Green (A) and Natural (B)
- Pair of 3.25mm (US 3) needles

SKIRT

With A, cast on 78 sts.
Row 1 (RS): K3, yo, k1, k2tog, p1, ssk, k1, yo, k3; rep to end.
Row 2: K3, p3, k1, p3, k3; rep to end.
Row 3: As Row 1.
Row 4: As Row 2.
Row 5: K3, yo, k1, yo, k2tog, p1, ssk, yo, k4; rep to end.
Row 6: K4, p2, k1, p4, k3, rep to end.
Row 7: (K3, yo) twice, sk2po, yo, k5; rep to end.
Row 8: K5, p7, k3; rep to end.
Row 9: K3, yo, k5, yo, k7; rep to end.
Row 10: K4, k2tog, *k2, k2tog; rep from * to last 4 sts, k4.

Cont without shaping in St-st until work measures 17cm (6¾in). Cast off, leaving a long tail.

BODICE

With A, cast on 78 sts. Work 6 rows in St-st, ending on a RS. K 4 rows. Cast off.

SLEEVES (MAKE 2)

With A, cast on 22 sts. Work 3 rows in k1, p1 rib. Cont in St-st, at the same time inc 4 sts evenly over next row (26 sts). Work 5 rows in St-st. Cast off 2 sts at beg of next 2 rows (22 sts). K2tog at each end of foll row and foll alt rows until 12 sts rem. Cast off.

UNDERSKIRT

With B, cast on 18 sts. Work 4 rows in moss-st. Cont without shaping in St-st until work measures 17cm (6¾in). Cast off, leaving a long tail.

SHAWL COLLAR

With B, cast on 1 st.
Row 1: K.
Row 2 (and every even row): P.
Row 3: Kfb (2 sts).
Row 5: Kfb twice (4 sts).
Row 7: K1, kfb twice, k1 (6 sts).
Row 9: K1, kfb, k to last 2 sts, kfb, k1 (8 sts).
Row 10: P.
Rep last 2 rows until 50 sts rem. Cast off.

MAKING UP

Press all pieces lightly on WS using a warm iron over a damp cloth. Sew a running st along the cast-off edge of the main Skirt and gather until it fits the doll's waist. Sew a couple of back sts to secure and fasten off. Sew a running st along the cast-off edge of the Underskirt and pull tight. Sew the side edges of the Bodice to form a ring (the cast-off garter-st edge forms the top of the Bodice). Sew a running st along both edges of the Bodice and fit on to the doll and gather until it fits the doll's torso. Sew the Bodice to the Skirt, ensuring that the seam is at the centre back. Sew the Underskirt to the WS of the main Skirt, ensuring that there is a gap on the main Skirt for the Underskirt to show through. Put the dress on the doll and arrange the Shawl Collar so that the central point is tucked into the back of the dress, and the two edge points are tucked into the top of the Bodice. Sew around the bodice top. Sew the sleeve seams. Pull the Sleeves on to the doll so that they overlap the Shawl Collar. Sew a running st along the top of the sleeve caps and gather until they fit the arms. Sew around the edges of the sleeve caps to the Shawl Collar. Tuck the ribbed sleeve welts under slightly to form a puff. Darn in ends.

MISS BATES' SHAWL

MATERIALS

- 28g (1oz) Brown 3ply (light fingering) yarn (A)
- Scraps of green (or contrasting) 3ply (light fingering) yarn for fringe
- Pair of 3.25mm (US 3) needles

With A, cast on 1 st.

Row 1: K.
Row 2: Yo, k to end.
Rep row to 80 sts. Cast off.

MAKING UP

Press lightly on WS using a warm iron over a damp cloth. Darn in ends. Attach a fringe to the two side edges (see page 109).

MISS BATES' BONNET

MATERIALS

- 1 x 50g ball Patons Diploma Gold 4ply (fingering 55% wool/25% acrylic/20% nylon; 50g/201 yds) in shade 4200 Gold
- Pair of 3.25mm (US 3) needles
- Set of 4 x 3.25mm (US 3) dpns
- Small amount of thin ribbon

CROWN

With 3.25mm (US 3) dpns, cast on 6 sts. K 1 row, divide sts evenly between 3 dpns (2 sts on each needle), then proceed as follows:

Rnd 1 (RS): M1, k1; rep to end (12 sts).
Rnd 2 (and foll even rows): K.
Rnd 3: M1, k2; rep to end (18 sts).
Rnd 5: M1, k3; rep to end (24 sts).
Rnd 7: M1, k4; rep to end (30 sts).
Rnd 9: M1, k5; rep to end (36 sts).
Rnd 11: M1, k6; rep to end (42 sts).
Rnd 13: M1, k7; rep to end (48 sts).
Rnd 15: M1, k8; rep to end (54 sts).
Rnd 17: M1, k9; rep to end (60 sts).
Rnd 19: M1, k10; rep to end (68 sts).
Rnd 21: M1, k11; rep to end (74 sts). P2 rows. Cast off.

BRIM

With 3.25mm (US 3) needles, cast on 7 sts. Proceed in moss-st. Inc 1 st at each end of every row to 25 sts. Work 10 rows without shaping.
Next row (RS): Moss-st 10, turn.

Proceed on these 10 sts only.
Next row: K2tog, moss-st to end (8 sts). Dec 1 st at inner edge on every foll alt row until 5 sts rem. Work 3 rows without shaping.
Next row: K2tog, moss-st 3 (4 sts). Work 2 rows without shaping.
Next row: K2tog, moss-st 2 (3 sts). Work 1 row without shaping.
Next row: K2tog, moss-st 1 (2 sts).
Next row: K2tog, fasten off.
With RS facing, rejoin yarn to rem 15 sts. Cast off 5 sts, work to end. Follow instructions for first side, reversing shaping.

MAKING UP

Sew Brim to Crown, shaping it evenly around the edge. Cut two pieces of ribbon and sew them to the sides of the Crown. Darn in ends.

PICNIC BASKET

MATERIALS

- 1 x 50g ball 3ply Natural Jute Twine (approx. 50g/131yds)
- Small amount of dark brown DK or Aran yarn (for toggles and handle)
- Pair of 3.75mm (US 5) needles
- Small amount of gingham fabric (optional)
- Small amount of white 4ply (fingering) yarn (for plate)

BASE AND LID (BOTH ALIKE)

Cast on 16 sts. Cont in garter-st until work measures 6.25cm (2½in). Cast off.

SIDES (MADE IN ONE PIECE)

Cast on 52 sts. Cont in garter-st until work measures 2.5cm (1in). Cast off.

PLATE

With white 4ply (fingering) yarn and only using 1 strand, follow instructions for Cake Top and Bottom (see page 64) until you reach 18 sts. Rep last 2 rnds once more (27 sts).
Next rnd: P.
Next rnd: Pfb, p2; rep to end (36 sts).
Next rnd: P.
Cast off.

MAKING UP

Sew the side edges together to form a ring. Sew the Base to the Sides. Pinch the corners of the Sides slightly and sew to form a sharper edge. Attach the Lid to the Sides using the brown yarn to form hinges. Work 3.75cm (1½in) of I-cord (see page 108) with the brown yarn and attach to the front of the basket. Make two bobbles either side with the brown yarn by sewing two large French knots (see page 108). Sew two loops to the Lid to correspond to the bobbles. Darn in ends. Line the basket Lid with gingham fabric by cutting the fabric slightly larger than the basket Lid and pressing the edges under, then sew to the Lid. Press and starch the Plate; darn in ends. With dark brown yarn, sew 2 crossed straps to the gingham to hold the plate (see image).

PICNIC BLANKET

MATERIALS

- 2 x 50g balls Rowan Pure Wool DK (100% wool; 50g/136yds) in shade 013 Enamel

- Pair of 4mm (US 6) needles
- 4mm (G/6) crochet hook (optional)

Cast on 84 sts. Work 4 rows in garter-st, then proceed in patt as follows:

Row 1 (WS): K4, p to last 4 sts, k4.
Row 2: K6, *yf, k2, sl1, k1, psso, k2tog, k2, yf, k1; rep from * to last 6 sts, k6.
Row 3: Rep Row 1.
Row 4: K5, *yf, k2, sl1, k1, psso, k2tog, k2, yf, k1; rep from * to last 7 sts, k7.

Cont in patt until work measures 36.75cm (14½in). Work 4 rows in garter-st. Cast off.

MAKING UP

Press lightly on WS using a warm iron over a damp cloth. Darn in ends.
Optional Crochet Shell Edging: With the crochet hook, starting at one corner, join the yarn to the blanket. *Make 5 tr into 1 edge st, then a little further along make a sl st into the edge; rep from * to end, working evenly as you go.

CAKE

MATERIALS

- 1 x 50g ball Red Heart Baby (100% acrylic; 50g/207yds) in each of shades 8528 Cream (MC) and 8505 Red (CC)
- Pair of 3.25mm (US 3) needles
- Set of 4 x 3.25mm (US 3) dpns
- Small amount of thin cardboard
- Small amount of toy stuffing

SIDES

With 3.25mm (US 3) needles and MC, cast on 10 sts.

Row 1 (WS): K4MC, p1CC, k1CC, k4MC.
Row 2: P4MC, k1CC, p1CC, p4MC.
Rep these 2 rows until work measures 19cm (7½in). Cast off.

TOP AND BOTTOM (BOTH ALIKE)
With 2 x 3.25mm (US 3) dpns cast on 1 st.
Next row (WS): K1, p1, k1 into st (3 sts).
Next row: P.
Next row: Kfb to end (6 sts). Distribute sts evenly over 3 dpns (2 sts per dpn) and cont to work in the rnd.
Next rnd: P.
Next rnd: Kfb to end (12 sts).
Next rnd: K.
Next rnd: Kfb, k1; rep to end (18 sts).
Next rnd: K.
Next rnd: Kfb, k2; rep to end (24 sts).
Next rnd: K.
Next rnd: Kfb, k3; rep to end (30 sts).

Next rnd: K.
Next rnd: Kfb, k4; rep to end (36 sts).
Next rnd: K.
Next rnd: Kfb, k5; rep to end (42 sts).
Cast off.

MAKING UP

Press pieces lightly on WS using a warm iron over a damp cloth. With CC, sew several French knots (see page 108) on to the Top, evenly spaced for decoration. Sew the cast-on and cast-off edges of the Sides together. Sew the Top to the Sides. Cut a small piece of thin cardboard to fit the inner circumference of the Sides, tape the edges and insert into the cake. Stuff lightly with toy stuffing so that the cake bulges slightly at the Top. Sew the Bottom to the Sides. Darn in ends.

OTHER ITEMS FROM THE SCENE

MISS BATES' DRESS
Follow instructions for Elizabeth's Dress on page 46.

Wedding Bells for Emma and Mr Knightley

EMMA

'The wishes, the hopes, the confidence, the predictions of the small band of true friends who witnessed the ceremony, were fully answered in the perfect happiness of the union.'

A pattern runs through Jane Austen's books – although the path of true love never runs smoothly, the heroine always ends up getting her man, so here's a toast to Miss Emma Woodhouse and Mr George Knightley.

The outcome was never a sure thing; there was a time when Mr Knightley was jealous of Frank Churchill and perceived him as a serious threat to his relationship with Emma. At one point Harriet confessed to Emma that she was developing feelings for Mr Knightley and that she had hopes of her feelings being reciprocated. As you can imagine, Emma bitterly regretted ever having raised Harriet's hopes, but this last complication was the tipping point for Emma and made her realise that she was in love with him herself, despite the fact that Emma had previously vowed never to marry. As soon as Harriet confides her feelings to Emma, we are told, *'It darted through her, with the speed of an arrow, that Mr Knightley must marry no one but herself!'*

When news is received that Frank Churchill is engaged to Jane Fairfax, Mr Knightley takes Emma to one side to comfort her. Of course, he has an ulterior motive and his concern is rewarded – in typically restrained style, they reveal their true feelings for each other. A date is set, and here they are on their special day. According to the unbearable Mrs Elton, the wedding is a humble affair compared with her own high expectations, but the reader is left in no doubt that it is a happy occasion, full of friends, good wishes and joy.

EMMA'S WEDDING DRESS

Follow instructions for Jane's Ball Gown on page 32, with the following addition:

BANDEAU

Cast on 24 sts.
Row 1 (RS): K2, *yo, sl1, k2, psso the 2 k sts; rep from * to last st, k1.
Rows 2 and 4: P.
Row 3: K1, *sl1, k2, psso the 2 k sts, yo; rep from * to last 2 sts, k2.
Rep these 4 rows 3 more times.
Cast off.

VEIL

Cast on 36 sts. Cont in 4 rows of st patt from Bandeau until work measures 12.75cm (5in) or desired length.

MAKING UP

Follow making up instructions for Jane's Ball Gown on page 32, with the following addition. Fold the Bandeau in half to establish the middle. Wrap a length of yarn around the middle of the Bandeau and secure. Sew the Bandeau to the dress bust. Darn in ends. Attach a small decoration to the centre of the Bandeau if required. For the Veil, sew a running st along one of the narrow sides and gather tightly. Attach to the hair with some decorative pins.

VICAR'S SURPLICE

MATERIALS

• 1 x 50g ball Scheepjeswol Cotton 8 (100% cotton; 50g/185yds) in shade 502 White
• Pair of 3.25mm (US 3) needles
• 3 stitch holders

TENSION

28 sts and 32 rows = 10cm (4in) over St-st

Cast on 49 sts.
Work 4 rows in moss-st. Cont in St-st until work measures 2.5cm (1in).
Next row: K1, p1, k1 (creates moss-st sleeve edge), kfb, k to last 3 sts, kfb, p1, k1 (51 sts).
Next row: K1, p1, k1, p to last 3 sts, k1, p1, k1.
Rep last 2 rows to 113 sts.

LEFT NECK

Next row: K1, p1, k46 sts, turn (place rem sts on to a st-holder).
Next row: P2tog, p to to last 3 sts, k1, p1, k1 (47 sts).
Next row: K1, p1, k to last 2 sts, k2tog (46 sts).
Rep last 2 rows (dec 1 st at neck edge and maintaining moss-st sleeve edge) until 42 sts rem, ending on a WS. Work 2 rows.
Next row: K1, p1, k to last st, kfb (43 sts).
Next row: P to last 3 sts, k1, p1, k1.
Rep last 2 rows to 48 sts, ending on a WS. Slip rem 46 sts on to a st-holder. Break yarn.

RIGHT NECK

With RS facing, rejoin yarn to rem 65 sts on st-holder, Cast off 17 sts, k to last 2 sts, p1, k1 (48 sts).
Next row: K1, p1, k1, p to last 2 sts, p2tog (47 sts).
Next row: K2tog, k to last 2 sts, p1, k1 (46 sts).
Rep last 2 rows (dec 1 st at neck edge and maintaining moss-st sleeve edge) until 42 sts rem,

ending on a RS. Work 2 rows.
Next row: Kfb, k to last 2 sts, p1, k1 (43 sts).
Next row: K1, p1, k1, p to end.
Rep last 2 rows to 48 sts, ending on a WS. Slip rem 48 sts on to a st-holder. Break yarn.
With RS facing, rejoin yarn to 48 sts of Right Neck (first st-holder) and k, cast on 17 sts, k across 48 sts of Left Neck, at the same time maintaining moss-st sleeve edges (113 sts).
Next row: K1, p1, k2tog, k to last 4 sts, k2tog, p1, k1 (111 sts).
Next row: K1, p1, k1, p to last 3 sts, k1, p1, k1.
Rep last 2 rows until 49 sts rem. Cont in St-st without shaping and without moss-st borders for 2.5cm (1in) more, ending on a WS. Work 4 rows in moss-st. Cast off.

MAKING UP

Press pieces lightly on WS using a warm iron over a damp cloth. Join the shoulder seams. Join the short side seams.

BIBLE

MATERIALS

- Small amount of 4ply (fingering) black cotton yarn (A)
- Small amount of 4ply (fingering) white cotton yarn (B)
- Small amount of 4ply (fingering) gold yarn (C)
- Pair of 3.25mm (US 3) needles

COVER

With A, cast on 21 sts. Work 4 rows in moss-st.

Next row (RS): K1, p1, k6, moss-st to end.

Next row: Moss-st 12, p6, k1, p1, k1. Rep last 2 rows until work measures 4.5cm (1¾in). Work 4 rows in moss-st. Cast off.

OUTER PAGE

With B, cast on 17 sts. Work in garter-st until work measures 4.5cm (1¾in). Cast off.

INNER PAGE

With B, cast on 15 sts. Work as for Outer Page.

MAKING UP

Press pieces lightly on WS using a warm iron over a damp cloth, applying starch to stiffen up the pieces. Sew the middle of the Outer Page to the Cover vertically along the middle using A. Sew the middle of the Inner Page to the Outer Page vertically along the middle using B. With C, embroider a cross to the Cover in the St-st section, using duplicate st (see page 108). Darn in ends.

BOUQUET

MATERIALS

- Small amount of green 4ply (fingering) or DK yarn in varying shades

- Small amount of 4ply (fingering) or DK yarn in appropriate colours for flowers (the bouquet in the picture features cream, lilac and pink)
- Small amount of thin cardboard
- Small amount of thin ribbon

Cut the cardboard to measure approx. 5 x 5cm (2 x 2in). Wrap the yarns around the cardboard as you would for a pom-pom, varying the colours evenly (NB: use every colour except one standout colour, which will be added at the final stage). Don't wrap too thickly or you'll end up with a fluffy pom-pom!

Cut the ends of the yarn and wrap tightly around the middle with a separate piece of yarn, tying to secure. Fluff out the top of the bouquet, fraying some of the ends here and there. Thread a needle with a length of the standout colour, tie a knot in the end and thread through the bouquet so that the knot sits at the top among the rest of the 'flowers'. Repeat several times. If desired, cut the brighter coloured yarns at the bottom of the bouquet so that only the green yarn representing the stalks is visible. Tie the ribbon in a bow around the middle.

OTHER ITEMS FROM THE SCENE

KNIGHTLEY'S TAILCOAT
Follow instructions for Darcy's
Tailcoat on page 33.

KNIGHTLEY'S WAISTCOAT
See page 18. Use yarn option 3.

LADIES' SHOES
See page 19.

KNIGHTLEY'S SHIRT
See page 17. Use yarn option 1.

VICAR'S TUNIC
Follow instructions on page 42.

DOVE
Follow instructions for Dove on
page 57.

KNIGHTLEY'S BREECHES
See page 16. Use yarn option 2.

VICAR'S CRAVAT
Follow instructions for Cravat on
page 18, using a small amount of
black 4ply (fingering) yarn.

KNIGHTLEY'S BOOTS
See page 17. Use yarn option 1.

VICAR'S BOOTS
See page 17. Use yarn option 2.

Mr Willoughby Rescues Marianne in the Rain

SENSE AND SENSIBILITY

'His manly beauty and more than common gracefulness were instantly the theme of general admiration.'

Poor Marianne Dashwood: out walking in the rain on a sheep-strewn moor, she has just fallen over and sprained her ankle. And the dashing gentleman coming to her rescue? But we're jumping ahead. When we first encounter them, the Dashwood sisters, Elinor and Marianne (along with their mother and youngest sister, Margaret), are in poor spirits. They receive bad news when the elderly Mr Dashwood dies and leaves his entire Sussex estate to John Dashwood, his insensitive son from a previous marriage. They are forced to move to the much humbler Barton Cottage in Devonshire, where they are welcomed to the area by Sir John Middleton, a lively relative.

Here the ladies meet the grave Colonel Brandon at a social occasion, and he's pegged as a prospective suitor for Marianne. Yet she is decidedly unimpressed, viewing him as *'old enough to be MY father'*. She sets her sights on a much more romantic scenario, so who can blame her for literally getting carried away by the handsome young gentleman who comes to her rescue? Even Mrs Dashwood and Elinor are impressed by John Willoughby's good looks and charm. He's Marianne's dream come true, and it soon becomes apparent that the feeling is mutual. Elinor, who thinks highly of Colonel Brandon, notices that his nose is distinctly put out of joint by Willoughby's arrival on the scene. Willoughby and Marianne mock Brandon in private, but could there be something more to Brandon's disapproval of Willoughby?

The young lovers display such a degree of intimacy that everybody believes an announcement of their engagement must be forthcoming. But it is not to be.

MARIANNE'S COAT

MATERIALS

- 1 x 50g ball Drops Alpaca (100% alpaca, 50g/167m) in each of shades 3800 Lilac (MC) and 4400 Dark Purple (CC)
- Pair of 3.25mm (US 3) needles

TENSION

38 sts and 58 rows = 10cm (4in) over patt

BACK

With CC, cast on 50 sts.
Row 1 (RS): K1, sl1 wyif; rep to end.
Row 2: P2, *sl1 wyib, p1; rep from * to last 2 sts, p2.
These 2 rows form patt. Work 4 more rows in patt. Change to MC and cont in patt, at the same time dec 1 st at each end of 2nd and every foll 11th row to 34 sts. Cont without shaping until work measures 16.5cm (6½in). Inc 1 st at each end of next row (36 sts). Work 4 more rows, ending on a WS.

Armhole

Next row: Cast off 3 sts at beg of next 2 rows (30 sts). Dec 1 st at each end of next row (28 sts). Cont without shaping until Armhole measures 4.5cm (1¾in). Cast off.

RIGHT FRONT

With CC, cast on 34 sts. Work 6 rows in patt.
Next row (RS): Work 4 sts in C, work to end in MC.
Next row: Work to last 4 sts in MC, work 4 sts in CC.
Cont to work in patt, with 4 sts in CC at button-band edge, at the same time dec 1 st at outer edge on 2nd and every foll 11th row until 18 sts rem. Cont without shaping until work measures 16.5cm (6½in).
Next row: Work 4 sts in CC, work to last st in MC, kfb (19 sts).
Work 5 more rows, ending on a RS.

Armhole

Next row: Cast off 3 sts at beg of next row, cont to end of row in patt (16 sts).
Next row (RS): Work 5 sts in CC, work to end in MC.
Next row: Work to last 5 sts in MC, work 5 sts in CC.
Next row: Work 6 sts in CC, work to end in MC.
Next row: Work to last 6 sts in MC, work 6 sts in CC.
Cont in patt, at the same time work 1 extra st in CC at the lapel edge on every even row until 9 sts in CC at the

lapel edge are worked. Cont in patt without shaping until Armhole measures 4.5cm (1¾in), ending on a RS.
Next row: Cast off 7 sts in MC for shoulder, cont to work in patt in CC to end of row.
Cont to work in patt in CC on these rem 9 sts for back collar until work measures 2.5cm (1in) from cast-off shoulder edge. Cast off.

LEFT FRONT

Follow instructions for Right Front, reversing shapings and button-band edge.

SLEEVES (MAKE 2)

With CC, cast on 20 sts. Work 6 rows in patt. Change to MC, inc 1 st at each end of 2nd row and foll 8th row until you reach 32 sts. Cont without shaping until work measures 10cm (4in). Cast off 3 sts at beg of next 2 rows (26 sts). Dec 1 st at each end of next and every alt row until 10 sts rem. Cast off.

MAKING UP

Press lightly on WS using a warm iron over a damp cloth. Sew shoulder seams. Sew back collar seam and sew to Back. Sew side and sleeve seams. Sew Sleeves into armholes. Darn in ends.

ELINOR'S BONNET

MATERIALS

- 1 x 50g ball Red Heart Margareta (100% acrylic; 50g/281yds) in shade 01197 Camel
- Set of 4 x 3.25mm (US 3) dpns
- Pair of 3.25mm (US 3) needles
- Small piece of thin cardboard
- Sticky tape
- Small amount of thin ribbon
- Sewing needle

Using 3.25mm (US 3) dpns, cast on 1 st.
Next row: (K1, p1, k1) into st (3 sts).
Next row: P.
Next row: Kfb to end (6 sts).
Distribute sts evenly over 3 dpns (2 sts per dpn) and cont to work in the rnd.
Next rnd: P.

Next rnd: Kfb to end (12 sts).
Next rnd: K.
Next rnd: Kfb, k1; rep to end (18 sts).
Next rnd: K.
Next rnd: Kfb, k1; rep to end (27 sts).
Next rnd: K.
Next rnd: Kfb, k2; rep to end (36 sts).
Next rnd: P.
K 2 rnds. P 1 rnd. K 4 rnds. P 1 rnd. K 6 rnds. P 1 rnd.
Next rnd: K5, kfb; rep to end (42 sts).
Next rnd: K.

Next rnd: K6, kfb; rep to end (48 sts).
K 2 rnds.
Next rnd: (K7, kfb) 4 times, cast off 16 sts (36 sts).

BRIM
Change to 3.25mm (US 3) needles, rejoin yarn.
K 2 rows.
Next row: *K3, kfb; rep from * to last 4 sts, k4 (44 sts).
Cont to work in garter-st, at the same time dec 1 st at each end of next and every foll 4th row until 36 sts rem. Dec 1 st at each end of next 2 rows (32 sts). Cast off.

MAKING UP

Press Brim lightly on WS using a warm iron over a damp cloth. Cut out a thin rectangle of cardboard to fit inside the bonnet and tape to form a circle. Sew a piece of thin ribbon to each side of the bonnet. Darn in ends.

Marianne's Dress

MATERIALS

- 1 x 50g ball Debbie Bliss Rialto Lace (100% wool; 50g/390m) in each of shades 001 Ecru (A), 029 Leaf (B) and 026 Coral (C)
- Pair of 2.25mm (US 1) needles

TENSION

37 sts and 42 rows = 10cm (4in) over St-st

BACK AND FRONT (BOTH ALIKE)

With B, cast on 56 sts. Work 3 rows in St-st.
Next row: K1, *k2tog, yo; rep from * to last st, k1.
Work 6 rows in St-st.
Change to A, work 4 rows in St-st.
Row 1: K4A, work from chart to last 3 sts, k3A.

Cont to work from Chart until work measures 16.5cm (6½in) from colour change, ending on a Row 4 or 12 of chart. Work 2 rows in St-st.
Next row (RS): With A, k5, *k2tog, k2; rep from * to last 7 sts, k2tog, k5 (44 sts).
Work 7 rows in St-st.

Armhole
Cast off 3 sts at beg of next 2 rows (38 sts). K2tog at each end of next row (36 sts). Cont without shaping until Armhole measures 2cm (¾in).
Left shoulder
Next row (RS): K9, turn.
Next row: P2tog, p to end (8 sts). Cont in St-st, dec 1 st on WS rows at neck edge until 5 sts rem. Cast off. With RS facing, rejoin yarn to rem 27 sts. Cast off 18 sts, k to end. Cont on rem 9 sts, repeat left shoulder, but reverse shaping.

SLEEVES (MAKE 2)
With B, cast on 18 sts. Work 3 rows in St-st.
Next row: K1, *k2tog, yo; rep to last st, k1.
Work 4 rows in St-st, inc 1 st at each end of 2nd and 4th rows (22 sts).
Change to A and work 6 rows in St-st, inc 1 st at each end of 2nd and

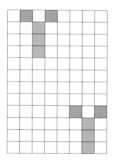

4th row. Cast off 3 sts at beg of next 2 rows. Dec 1 st at each end of every alt row until 6 sts rem. Cast off.

MAKING UP

Press lightly on WS using a warm iron over a damp cloth. Turn under and sew picot edge on dress sides and Sleeves. Sew shoulder and side seams. Sew sleeve seams and sew into armholes. Sew a running st around waist and neckline. Gather and secure to fit the doll. Darn in ends.

ELINOR'S DRESS

MATERIALS
- 1 x 50g ball Wendy Merino 4ply (fingering 100% wool; 50g/191yds) in each of shades 2376 Silver (MC) and 2365 Birch (CC)
- Pair of 3.25mm (US 3) needles

TENSION
30 sts and 56 rows = 10cm (4in) over patt

BACK
With MC, cast on 48 sts.
Row 1 (RS) (and every foll odd row): K.
Row 2: *K1, sl1 p'wise wyib; rep from * to last 2 sts, k2.
Row 3: K2, *sl1 p'wise wyib, k1; rep from * to end.
These 4 rows form the main skirt st pattern. Cont in patt until work measures 14.5cm (5¾in).
Next row: K2tog; rep to end of row (24 sts). Cont in St-st. **
Work 3 rows.
Next row (RS): Kfb, k to last st, kfb (26 sts).
Work 2 rows in St-st.
Armhole
Cast off 2 sts at each end of next 2 rows (22 sts). Dec 1 st at each end of next row (20 sts). Cont without shaping until Armhole measures 4.5cm (1¾in). Cast off.

FRONT
Rep instructions for Back to **.

Next row (WS): P.
Next row: K15, turn.
Next row: K1, p1, k1, p to end.
Next row: K13, p1, k1.
Next row: K1, p1, k1, p to end.
Armhole
Next row: Cast off 2 sts, k8, k2tog, k1, p1, k1 (12 sts).
Next row: K1, p1, k1, p to end.
Next row: K2tog, k8, p1, k1 (11 sts).
Next row: K1, p1, k1, p to end.
Next row: K6, k2tog, k1, p1, k1 (10 sts).
Work 3 rows.
Next row: K5, k2tog, k1, p1, k1 (9 sts).
Work 3 rows.
Next row: K4, k2tog, k1, p1, k1 (8 sts).
Work 1 row.
Next row: K3, k2tog, k1, p1, k1 (7 sts).
Next row: K1, p1, k2, p2tog, p1 (6 sts). Cast off and break yarn.
With RS facing, rejoin yarn to rem 9 sts.
Next row: Cast on 6 sts, k1, p1, k to end (15 sts).
Next row: P to last 3 sts, k1, p1, k1.
Next row: K1, p1, k to end.
Next row: P to last 3 sts, k1, p1, k1.
Next row: K1, p1, k1, skpo, k to end (13 sts).
Armhole
Cast off 2 sts, p to last 3 sts, k1, p1, k1 (12 sts).
Next row: K1, p1, k to last 2 sts, k2tog (11 sts).
Next row: P to last 3 sts, k1, p1, k1 (12 sts).
Next row: K1, p1, k1, skpo, k to end (10 sts).
Work 3 rows.
Rep last 4 rows once more then dec row again (8 sts).
Next row: K1, p1, k1, skpo, k to end (7 sts).
Next row: P to last 5 sts, p2tog, k1, p1, k1 (6 sts). Cast off.

SLEEVES (MAKE 2)
With CC, cast on 30 sts. Work 4 rows in moss-st.
Next row (RS): K2tog; rep to end (15 sts).
Next row: P.
Cont in St-st, at the same time inc 1 st at each end of 6th and every foll 8th row until you reach 21 sts. Cont without shaping until work measures 7.5cm (3in). Change to MC. Work 2 rows.
Next row: Kfb; rep to end (42 sts).
Next row: P.
Work 6 rows. Cast off 2 sts at beg of next 2 rows (38 sts). Dec 1 st at each end of next and foll alt rows until 28 sts rem. Dec 1 st at each end of every foll row until 22 sts rem. Cast off.

FRILL
With CC, cast on 6 sts.
Row 1 (RS): K1, k2tog, yo, k2, (yo) twice, k1.
Row 2: K1, (k1, p1) into double yo, k5 (8 sts).
Row 3: K1, k2tog, yo, k5.
Row 4: Cast off 2 sts, p1, p2tog, yo, k3 (6 sts).
Rep these 4 rows until frill matches bottom edge of skirt – approx. 38cm (15in). Cast off.

MAKING UP
Press lightly on WS with a warm iron over a damp cloth. Sew side and shoulder seams. Fit overlap of right side of bodice over left side and sew. Sew sleeve seams and sew a running st along top of Sleeves. Gather until they fit the armholes and secure. Sew Sleeves into armholes. Sew a running st around waist and neckline. Gather and secure to fit doll. Darn in ends. Puff top of Sleeves up so they slightly overhang the main Sleeve.

Willoughby's Riding Coat

MATERIALS

- 1 x 50g ball Phildar Phil Folk 50 (75% wool/25% nylon; 50g/229yds) in shade 0009 Lande
- Pair of 2.75mm (US 2) needles

Tension

27 sts and 34 rows = 10cm (4in) over moss-st

BACK

Tail

Cast on 25 sts. Work 3 rows in moss-st.

Next row: K1, p1, k1, p to end.
Next row: K to last 2 sts, p1, k1.
Next row: K1, p1, k1, p to end.
Next row: K2tog, k1, *p1, k3; rep from * to last 2 sts, p1, k1.
Next 3 rows: Cont in St-st, maintaining moss-st edge.

The last 4 rows form st patt. Cont in patt, dec 1 st at outer edge of every 7th row until 18 sts rem. Cont without shaping until work measures 14.5cm (5¾in), ending on a WS. Break yarn, place sts on to a st-holder.

Make another tail, reversing shaping.

With RS facing, place both tails on to one needle and work in patt across, omitting the moss-st edges (36 sts).

Cont in patt, maintaining dec rows on every 7th row until 34 sts rem.

Cont without shaping until work measures 17.75cm (7in).

Armhole

Cont in St-st. Cast off 2 sts at beg of next 2 rows (32 sts). K2tog at each end of foll row (30 sts). Cont without shaping until Armhole measures 7cm (2¾in). Cast off.

LEFT FRONT

Cast on 29 sts. Work 4 rows in moss-st.

Next row: K to last 2 sts, p1, k1.
Next row: K1, p1, k1, p to end.
Next row: K2tog, work in patt st to end.

Cont in patt st working moss-st button band, at the same time dec 1 st at outer edge every 7th row until 21 sts rem. Cont without shaping until work measures 17.75cm (7in) ending on a WS.

Armhole

Cont in St-st. Cast off 2 sts, k to end (19 sts).

Next row: K1, p1, k1, p to end.
Next row: K2tog, patt to last 4 sts, (p1, k1) twice) (18 sts).
Next row: K1, p1, k1, p to end.
Next row: K to last 4 sts, (p1, k1) twice.
Next row: (K1, p1) twice, k1, p to end.
Next row: K to last 6 sts, (p1, k1) to end.
Next row: (K1, p1) 3 times, k1, p to end.
Next row: K to last 6 sts, (p1, k1) to end.
Next row: (K1, p1) 4 times, k1, p to end.
Next row: K to last 8 sts, (p1, k1) to end.
Next row: (K1, p1) 4 times, k1, p to end.
Next row: K to last 8 sts, (p1, k1) to end.
Next row: Cast off 9 sts, p to end (9 sts).
Next row: K to last 2 sts, k2tog (8 sts).

Next row: P2tog, p to end (7 sts).
Next row: K to last 2 sts, k2tog (6 sts).

Work 3 rows in St-st. Cast off.

RIGHT FRONT

Work as for Left Front, reversing shapings.

SLEEVES

Cast on 25 sts. Work 4 rows in moss-st.

Rows 1–2: Work 2 rows in St-st.
Row 3: K2, *p1, k3; rep from * to last 3 sts, p1, k2.
Row 4: P.
Row 5: Inc 1 st at each end.

Cont in patt st, inc 1 st at each end of every foll 8th row until you reach 33 sts. Cont without shaping until work measures 10cm (4in) ending on a WS row.

Armhole

Cast off 2 sts at beg of next 2 rows. Dec 1 st at each end of next and foll alt rows until 13 sts rem. Cast off.

COLLAR

Cast on 5 sts. Work in moss-st for 15cm (6in). Cast off.

Making up

Press pieces lightly on WS using a warm iron over a damp cloth. Sew shoulder, side and sleeve seams then sew Sleeves into armholes. Fold back the lapels and secure with a couple of stitches. Pin the Collar on to the coat so that the centre Collar matches the centre Back, and the edges of the Collar reach the lapel. Sew to secure. Darn in ends.

SHEEP

MATERIALS

- 1 x 50g ball King Cole Merino Blend DK (100% wool; 50g/122yds) in each of shades 046 Aran (MC) and 048 Black (CC)
- Set of 4 x 4mm (US 6) dpns
- Pair of 4mm (US 6) needles
- Small amount of toy stuffing
- Armature wire or thick pipe cleaners

HEAD

With CC and 2 x 4mm (US 6) dpns, cast on 3 sts.
Row 1 (RS): Kfb to end (6 sts). Distribute sts evenly over 3 needles (2 sts per needle) and cont to work in the rnd.
Rnd 2: Kfb to end (12 sts).
Rnd 3: K.
Rnd 4: Kfb, k1; rep to end (18 sts).
Rnds 5–10: K 6 rows. Change to MC.

MAIN BODY

Rnd 11: Kfb 4 times, (k1, kfb) 5 times, kfb 4 times (31 sts).

Rnd 12 (and every foll even row): P.
Rnd 13: Kfb 5 times, k21, kfb 5 times (41 sts).
Rnd 15: Kfb 5 times, k31, kfb 5 times (51 sts).
Rnd 17: K.
Rnd 18: P.
Stuff the head.
Rep rnds 17–18 twelve times.
Next rnd: K2tog 5 times, k31, k2tog 5 times (41 sts).
Next rnd: P.
Next rnd: K2tog 5 times, k21, k2tog 5 times (31 sts).
Next rnd: P.
Next rnd: K2tog 5 times, k2, k2tog, k3, k2tog, k2, k2tog 5 times (19 sts).
Next rnd: P.
Stuff the body.
Next rnd: K2tog 4 times, k3, k2tog 4 times (11 sts).
Next rnd: K2tog, k1; rep to last 2 sts, k2tog (7 sts).
Stuff any gaps remaining in the body.

TAIL

Change to CC. K 6 rows.
Next rnd: K2tog, k3tog, k2tog (3 sts). P3tog, break yarn and draw through loop.

LEGS (MAKE 4)

Turn the sheep upside down and choose where you would like to position the 4 legs, marking with pins or pieces of thread. With CC and 4mm (US 6) dpns, pick up 9 sts from the Main Body of the sheep evenly in a circle around one of the markers to form a cylindrical leg. Cont to work in the rnd (every row k) until leg measures approx. 5cm (2in) or desired length. Cut a length of armature wire or thick pipe cleaner the length of the leg plus an extra 1.25cm (½in). Fold the ends of the wire/pipe cleaner to form a small loop and insert into the leg. Stuff the leg firmly around the wire/pipe cleaner.
Next rnd: K3tog to end (3 sts). K3tog, break yarn and draw end through loop.
Make 3 more legs around the remaining markers.

EARS

With CC and 4mm (US 6) needles, cast on 3 sts. K 1 row. Inc 1 st at each end of foll row (5 sts). Work 4 rows in garter-st. Dec 1 st at each end of foll row. K3tog. Cast off.

MAKING UP

Embroider eyes if desired, using French knots (see page 108) with a contrasting colour. Fold the cast-on edge of Ears slightly, pin to desired spot, and sew to secure. Darn in ends.

OTHER ITEMS FROM THE SCENE

WILLOUGHBY'S SHIRT
See page 17. Use yarn option 4.

WILLOUGHBY'S WAISTCOAT
See page 18. Use yarn option 1.

WILLOUGHBY'S BREECHES
See page 16. Use yarn option 3.

WILLOUGHBY'S BOOTS
See page 17. Use yarn option 2.

LADIES' SHOES
See page 19.

Colonel Brandon and Willoughby Fight a Duel

SENSE AND SENSIBILITY

'We met by appointment, he to defend,
I to punish his conduct.'

Although emotions often run high in Austen's books, her characters seldom come to blows. Remember the debonair Willoughby from the previous scene? Well, it's been revealed that he has a dark past. Suspicions arise when he behaves in a most ungentlemanly manner, denying that he had feelings for Marianne and becoming engaged to another, much wealthier lady. Marianne is heartbroken and eventually falls seriously ill. Meanwhile, Colonel Brandon reveals to Elinor the truth behind his antagonism towards Willoughby. When Brandon was young, he was in love with Eliza, an orphan entrusted to his father's care. Eliza was coerced into a loveless marriage with his brother, and when a grief-stricken Brandon returned three years later from his military adventures, he found her divorced and impoverished, with a three-year-old daughter, the result of a clandestine relationship. Eliza died, and Brandon promised to take care of her daughter, also called Eliza. At some point, Eliza Junior went to Bath and disappeared for eight months, during which it emerges that Willoughby seduced her and left her pregnant, utterly in disgrace. Reason enough to challenge him to a duel!

Fortunately, neither party is wounded, although we can imagine Willoughby's shameful defeat as the older man exerts his strength and experience. Elinor is a little rueful and *'sighed over the fancied necessity of this; but to a man and a soldier she presumed not to censure it'*. How will it all end? Well, you guessed it – a happy ending awaits both Dashwoods! Marianne recovers from her grief and sees Colonel Brandon in a new light, while Elinor is reunited with her true love, Edward Ferrars.

BRANDON'S AND WILLOUGHBY'S SHIRTS

MATERIALS

For Brandon's Shirt
- 2 x 25g balls Jamieson & Smith 2ply (light fingering, 100% Shetland wool; 25g/125yds) in shade 01A Cream

For Willoughby's Shirt
- 1 x 50g ball Bergere de France Coton Fifty (50% cotton/50% acrylic; 50g/153yds) in shade 22493 Coco

For both shirts
- Pair of 3.25mm (US 3) needles

TENSION

28 sts and 37 rows = 10cm (4in) over St-st

BACK

Cast on 45 sts. Work 3 rows in St-st. K 1 row (forms hem).** Cont without shaping in St-st until work measures 14cm (5½in). Cast off.

FRONT

Cast on 45 sts. Follow instructions for Back to **. Cont without shaping until work measures 5cm (2in), ending on a WS.
Next row: K21, p1, k1, p1, turn.
Next row: P1, k1, p to end.
***Cont on these 24 sts, working a moss-st button band until work measures 12.75cm (5in) ending on a RS.
Next row: Cast off 2 sts, p to end (22 sts).
Next row: K to last 2 sts, k2tog (21 sts).
Next row: P2tog, p to end (20 sts).
Next row: K to last 2 sts, k2tog (19 sts).
Next row: P2tog, p to end (18 sts). Cast off and break yarn.***
With RS facing, rejoin yarn to rem 21 sts. Cast on 3 sts (24 sts).
Next row: P1, k1, p1, k to end.
Next row: P to last 2 sts, k1, p1.
Follow instructions from *** to ***, reversing shaping for neck.

SLEEVES (MAKE 2)

Cast on 16 sts. Work 4 rows in moss-st.
Next row (RS): Kfb into every st (32 sts). Cont in St-st, at the same time inc 1 st at each end of every 8th row until you reach 42 sts. Cont

without shaping until work measures 12.75cm (5in). Cast off.

COLLAR

Cast on 7 sts. Work 2 rows in moss-st. Inc 1 st at beg of foll and next alt row (7 sts). Work in moss-st until work measures 11.5cm (4¼in), ending on a RS. Dec 1 st at beg of next and foll alt row (5 sts). Work 2 rows. Cast off.

BRANDON'S SHIRT FRILL

Cast on 36 sts. Work 4 rows in St-st. Break yarn, leaving a long tail; thread the tail through the sts while still on the needle and pull them off, gathering slightly to fit the button-band edge, and secure.

MAKING UP

Press all pieces lightly on WS using a warm iron over a damp cloth. Sew a running st along the top of the Back and gather until it measures 11.5cm (4½in). Sew a running st along the top of the Front shoulders until they each measure 2.5cm (1in). Sew a running st along the sleeve tops until they each measure 11.5cm (4½in). Sew the overlap button band so that the right button band fits under the left button band. Sew side seams – they should measure 5.75cm (2¼in). Sew sleeve seams, then sew Sleeves into armholes. Sew Collar to shirt. Sew the Frill to the left button band of Brandon's shirt. Darn in ends.

BRANDON'S WAISTCOAT

MATERIALS

- 1 x 50g ball Red Heart Margareta (sportweight, 100% acrylic; 50g/281yds) in shade 0534 Claret-Red
- Pair of 3.25mm (US 3) needles
- 4 small gold beads

TENSION

28 sts and 34 rows = 10cm (4in) over moss-st

BACK

Cast on 33 sts. Work in moss-st until work measures 3.75cm (1½in).

Armhole

Cast off 2 sts at beg of next 2 rows (29 sts). Dec 1 st at each end of next and foll alt row (25 sts). Cont without shaping until Armhole measures 6.25cm (2½in). Cast off.

LEFT FRONT

Cast on 21 sts. Cont in moss-st until work measures 3.75cm (1½in), ending on a RS.

Armhole

Cast off 2 sts at beg of next row (19 sts). Dec 1 st at end of next and foll alt row (17 sts). Cont until Armhole measures 4.5cm (1¾in) ending on a RS.

Next row: Cast off 7 sts, moss-st to end.

Dec 1 st at neck edge of next 5 rows (5 sts). Cast off.

RIGHT FRONT

Follow instructions for Left Front, reversing shaping.

COLLAR

Cast on 7 sts. Cont in moss-st until work measures 14.5cm (5¾in). Cast off.

MAKING UP

Press pieces on WS with a warm iron over a damp cloth. Sew side and shoulder seams. Overlap the Left Front over the Right Front slightly and sew to secure. Sew on beads to Left Front at even intervals. Fold back the lapels and sew to secure. Pin the Collar on to the coat so that the centre Collar matches the centre Back, and the edges of the Collar reach the lapel. Sew to secure. Darn in ends.

SWORDS

MATERIALS

- 1 x 50g ball Anchor Artiste Metallic (80% viscose/20% polyester; 50g/109yds) in shade 301 Silver (MC)
- Small amount of black 4ply (fingering) yarn (CC)
- Pair of 3.25mm (US 3) needles
- Pipe cleaners or small amount of armature wire
- Small amount of thin cardboard
- Small amount of toy stuffing or cotton wool

With MC, cast on 1 st.

BLADE

Row 1: (K1, p1, k1) into st (3 sts).
Row 2 (and foll even rows): P.
Row 3: Kfb, sl1 p'wise, kfb (5 sts).
Row 5: K2, sl1 p'wise, k2.
Row 7: Kfb, k1, sl1 p'wise, k1, kfb (7 sts).
Row 9: K3, sl1 p'wise, k3.
Row 10: P.
Rep last 2 rows until work measures 11.5cm (4½in).

HILT

Change to CC.
Next row: K2tog, k to end (6 sts).
Next row: P.
Next row: K2tog to end (3 sts).
Next row: P.
Next row: Kfb to end (6 sts).
Next row: P.
Next row: K1, kfb; rep to end (9 sts).
Next row: P.
Next row: Change to CC, k.
Next row: P.

Next row: K1, k2tog; rep to end (6 sts).
Next row: P.
Next row: K2tog to end (3 sts). Break yarn, thread yarn through rem 3 sts and draw up.

GUARD

With MC, cast on 9 sts.
Row 1: Kfb to end (18 sts).
Row 2 (and foll even rows): K.
Row 3: Kfb, k1; rep to end (27 sts).
Row 5: Kfb, k2; rep to end (36 sts).
Row 6: Kfb, k3; rep to end (45 sts).
K 2 rows. Cast off.

MAKING UP

Press piece lightly on WS using a warm iron over a damp cloth. Fold the sword in half and cut a piece of thin cardboard the shape and size of the folded fabric, tapering it off at the top where the CC Hilt starts. Fold the knitted fabric around the cardboard and oversew along the Blade with MC. Cut a piece of wire

or pipe cleaner the entire length of the sword plus an extra 6mm (¼in). Fold the top over into a small loop and push the end to the end of the sword. Sew the CC part of the Hilt, then stuff a little to push the top out into a rounded shape. Finish sewing the top with CC. Darn in ends. Sew the guard side seam, leaving a small hole in the middle.

Push the Guard over the Hilt so that it rests at the top of the blade. Sew to secure. Darn in ends.

OTHER ITEMS FROM THE SCENE

WILLOUGHBY'S BREECHES
See page 16. Use yarn option 3.

BRANDON'S BREECHES
See page 16. Use yarn option 2.

WILLOUGHBY'S BOOTS
See page 17. Use yarn option 1.

BRANDON'S BOOTS
See page 17. Use yarn option 2.

ANNE AND CAPTAIN WENTWORTH MEET AGAIN AT UPPERCROSS

PERSUASION

'Eight years, almost eight years had passed, since all had been given up.'

What could be more charming than this little scenario? A lady entertains a gentleman at the pianoforte. But there are underlying currents at play. The lady is Anne Elliot, the daughter of Sir Walter Elliot, master of Kellynch Hall in Somerset, who has recently had to accept that his fortunes are not what they once were. The family has moved to modest accommodation in Bath, and Kellynch Hall has been let to Admiral Croft.

It turns out that Anne was once in love with Mrs Croft's brother, Captain Frederick Wentworth. Unfortunately, her father decided the relationship was not meant to be, and persuaded Anne that the fortuneless Mr Wentworth, as he was at the time, was certainly no match for an Elliot. Mr Wentworth gloomily left the country to make his fortune in the navy, and Anne never fully recovered from the loss of her love.

Fast-forward eight years, and fate has brought them together once again. Wentworth has never forgiven Anne and he remains resentful over their separation: '*She had given him up to oblige others. It had been the effect of over-persuasion. It had been weakness and timidity.*' Now he's on the hunt for a suitable wife: '*any pleasing young woman who came his way, excepting Anne Elliot*'. The former lovers often attend the same dinners, and although we witness many awkward moments of cold politeness, we may also imagine a repressed intimacy – times when Captain Wentworth remembers his youthful attraction to Anne Elliot. In the end, Captain Wentworth forgets his pride and declares, '*You pierce my soul. I am half agony, half hope … I have loved none but you.*'

ANNE'S DRESS

MATERIALS

- 1 x 50g ball Drops Alpaca (100% alpaca; 50g/183yds) in shade 7120 Light Greyish Green
- Pair of 3.25mm (US 3) needles

TENSION

28 sts and 32 rows = 10cm (4in) over St-st.

FRONT AND BACK (BOTH ALIKE)

Cast on 48 sts.

Row 1 (RS): P.

Row 2: K.

Row 3: P6, *cast on 8 sts, k those 8 cast-on sts, p6; rep from * to end.

Rows 4 and 6: K6, *p8, k6; rep from * to end.

Row 5: P6, *k8, p6; rep from * to end.

Row 7: P6, *ssk, k4, k2tog, p6; rep from * to end.

Row 8: K6, *p6, k6; rep from * to end.

Row 9: P6, *ssk, k2, k2tog, p6; rep from * to end.

Row 10: K6, *p4, k6; rep from * to end.

Row 11: P6, *ssk, k2tog; rep from * to end.

Row 12: K6, *p2, k6; rep from * to end.

Row 13: P6, *k2tog, p6; rep from * to end.

Row 14: K6, *p1 tbl, k6; rep from * to end.

Row 15: P6, *k1 tbl, p6; rep from * to end (55 sts).

You now have 55 sts. Rep rows 14 and 15 until work measures 16.5cm (6½in).

Next row: P1, *p2tog; rep from * to end (28 sts).

Work 5 rows in rev St-st.

Armhole

Cast off 2 sts at beg of next 2 rows (24 sts). Dec 1 st at each end of next row (22 sts). Cont without shaping until Armhole measures 2.5cm (1in), ending on a WS.

Next row (RS): P8, turn.

Next row: K2tog, k to end (7 sts).

Next row: P to last 2 sts, p2tog (6 sts).

Next row: K2tog, k to end (5 sts). Work 1 row. Cast off.

With RS facing, rejoin yarn to rem 14 sts.

Next row: Cast off 6 sts, p8 (8 sts).

Next row: K to last 2 sts, k2tog (7 sts).

Next row: P2tog, p to end (6 sts).

Next row: K to last 2 sts, k2tog (5 sts).

Work 1 row. Cast off.

MAKING UP

Press lightly on WS using a warm iron over a damp cloth. Sew shoulder seams. Sew side seams. Sew a running thread around the waist, gather to fit waist and secure. Darn in ends.

ANNE'S OVERDRESS

MATERIALS

- 1 x 50g ball Drops Alpaca (100% alpaca; 50g/183yds) in shade 7139 Dark Greyish Green
- Pair of 3.25mm (US 3) needles
- 1 small bead

TENSION

28 sts and 32 rows = 10cm (4in) over St-st.

BACK

Cast on 45 sts. Work 4 rows in moss-st. Cont in St-st until work measures 16.5cm (6½in), ending on a WS.

Next row (RS): K1, (k2tog) to end (23 sts). Work 2 rows.

Next row: Inc 1 st at each end (25 sts). Work 2 rows.

Armhole

Cast off 2 sts at beg of next 2 rows (21 sts). Dec 1 st at each end of next row (19 sts). Cont in St-st until Armhole measures 4.5cm (1¾in). Cast off.

RIGHT FRONT

Cast on 29 sts. Work 4 rows in moss-st. Cont in St-st until work measures 16.5cm (6½in), ending on a WS.

Next row: Cast on 6 sts, moss-st 9, (k2 tog) to end (22 sts).

Next row: P13, moss-st to end.

Next row: Moss-st 9, k to end.

Next row: Pfb, p12, moss-st 9 (23 sts).
Next row: Cast off 6 sts, k to end (17 sts).
Next row: P to last 2 sts, p2tog (16 sts).
Next row: K2tog, k to end (15 sts).
Armhole
Next row: Cast off 2 sts, p to last 2 sts, p2tog (12 sts).
Next row: K2tog, k to end (11 sts).
Next row: P2tog, p to end (10 sts).
K2tog at beg of next and foll alt rows until 6 sts rem. Cont without shaping until Armhole measures

4.5cm (1¾in). Cast off.
LEFT FRONT
Follow instructions for Right Front, reversing shapings.

SLEEVES (MAKE 2)
Cast on 15 sts. Work 4 rows in moss-st. Cont in St-st, inc 1 st at each end of 5th and every foll 9th row to 23 sts. Cast off 2 sts at beg of next 2 rows (19 sts). Dec 1 st at each end of next and every foll alt row until 5 sts rem. Cast off.

MAKING UP
Press lightly on WS using a warm iron over a damp cloth. Sew shoulder and side seams. Sew sleeve seams and sew in sleeves, gathering the tops slightly if necessary to fit. Sew a running st around the waist, gather to fit waist and secure. Overlap the fronts at the waist, sew on bead for a button. Darn in ends.

PIANOFORTE

MATERIALS

- 1 x 50g ball Scheepjeswol Cotton 8 (100% cotton; 50g/185yds) in each of shades 657 Dark Brown (A), 659 Light Brown (B), 502 White (C) and 515 Black (D)
- Pair of 3.25mm (US 3) needles
- Set of 4 x 3.25mm (US 3) dpns
- 3 stitch holders
- Thin cardboard
- Sticky tape (e.g., duct tape)
- Cocktail stick

TENSION

26 sts and 34 rows = 10cm (4in) over St-st

FRONT

With 3.25mm (US 3) needles and A, cast on 70 sts. Work 6 rows in St-st (ending on a WS).
Next row (RS): K21, place rem 49 sts on to st-holder.

Cont on these 21 sts in St-st until work measures 6.25cm (2½in) ending on a RS.
K 1 row.
Next row (RS): Cast on 18 sts, moss-st 18, k21 (39 sts).
Next row: P21, moss-st 18.
Next row: Moss-st 18, k21.
Rep last 2 rows until work measures 9cm (3½in), ending on a WS. Place sts on to st-holder.
With RS facing, return to rem 49 sts. Keep next 41 sts on st-holder, rejoin yarn to rem last 8 sts. Cont on these 8 sts in St-st until work measures 6.25cm (2½in) ending on a RS.
Next row: Cast on 18 sts, moss-st 18, p8 (26 sts).
Next row: K8, moss-st 18.
Rep last 2 rows until work measures 9cm (3½in), ending on a WS. Place sts on to st-holder.

KEYBOARD

With RS facing, return to 41 sts on st-holder, join in C. Work 3 rows in St-st. K 1 row. Work 4 rows in St-st.
Next row: K3C, *(k1D, k1C) 3 times, k1C, (k1D, k1C) twice, k1C; rep from * twice more, k2C.
Next row: P the white sts, k the black sts.
Next row: K the white sts, p the black sts.
Next row: P the white sts, k the black sts.

BACK BOARD AND SIDE BOARDS

Next row: Join in B, cast on 8 sts, k8, sl1 wyib, k39, sl1 wyib (49 sts).
Next row: Cast on 8 sts, p10, (k1, p1) to last 10 sts, k1, p9 (57 sts).
Next row: K8, sl1 wyib, moss-st to last 9 sts, sl1 wyib, k8.
Rep last 2 rows until Back Board measures 3cm (1¼in), then rep WS row once.
Next row: Cast off 8 sts, k40, sl1 wyib, k8 (49 sts).
Next row: Cast off 8 sts, k to end (41 sts). Break yarn.

TOP

Next row: With RS facing, sl 39 sts from 1st st-holder on to a needle, rejoin A, moss-st 18, k21, k across 41 sts from 3rd st-holder, sl 26 sts from 2nd st-holder on to needle, then k8, moss-st 18 (106 sts).
Next row: Moss-st 18, p70, moss-st 18.
Next row: Moss-st 18, k70, moss-st 18.
Rep last 2 rows until Top measures 10cm (4in) from cast-on side sts, ending on a WS.
Next row: Cast off 18 sts, k70, moss-st 18 (88 sts).
Next row: Cast off 18 sts, p to end (70 sts).

BACK

Cont in moss-st until Back measures 6.25cm (2½in), ending on a RS.
K 1 row.

BASE

Cont in St-st until Base measures 10cm (4in). Cast off.

LEGS (MAKE 4)

With 2 x 3.25mm (US 3) dpns and A, cast on 1 st.
Next row: (K1, p1, k1) into st (3 sts).
Next row: K.
Next row: Kfb to end (6 sts).
Distribute sts evenly over 3 dpns (2 sts per needle) and cont in the rnd. Cont to k every rnd until work measures 2.5cm (1in).
Next rnd: (Kfb, k1) to end (9 sts). Cont to k every rnd until work measures 5cm (2in).
Next rnd: (Kfb, k2) to end (12 sts). Cont until work measures 7.5cm (3in).
Next rnd: (Kfb, k3) to end (15 sts). Cont until work measures 11.5cm (4½in). Cast off.

MUSIC STAND

With 3.25mm (US 3) needles and B, cast on 23 sts.
Row 1: K3, *sl1 p'wise, k1, yo, pass sl st over knitted st and yo, k3; rep from * to end.
Row 2: P.
Rep Rows 1 and 2 until work measures 5cm (2in), ending on a

RS. K1 row. Change to A. Cont in patt until work measures 10cm (4in). Cast off.

MAKING UP

Cut out cardboard inner frame, following the diagram. Tape together the base, sides, front and top to form a box. Tape the Back Board, Keyboard and Side Boards together separately, then insert into the open side of the main piano, and tape.
Press knitted pieces lightly on WS using a warm iron over a damp cloth. Sew the Keyboard to the Side Boards. Sew the Side Boards to the appropriate part of the Top. Sew the Side Boards to the Front and Keyboard front. Sew the cast-on edge of the moss-stitched Sides to the Front, and the cast-off edge to the Back. Sew the Base to the

moss-stitched sides. Sew the cast-off edge of the Base to the Front.
Cut 4 pieces of cardboard per the diagram for the Legs. Roll them into a cone shape so that they fit the inside of the knitted Leg pieces. Sew the legs slightly inset from the edge of each corner of the Pianoforte Base.
Cut a piece of cardboard per the diagram for the Music Stand. Fold the knitted music stand in half, with the lighter brown facing the front. Insert the cardboard and sew the remaining seam. Sew the Music Stand to the Pianoforte Top approx. 2.5cm (1in) away from the edge, making sure it sits in the middle of the keyboard width. Use a broken cocktail stick to prop up the stand. Darn in ends.

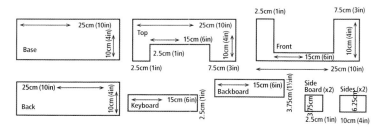

Piano Stool

MATERIALS

- 1 x 50g ball Scheepjeswol Cotton 8 (100% cotton; 50g/185yds) in each of shades 657 Dark Brown (MC) and 501 Natural (CC)
- Pair of 3.25mm (US 3) needles
- Set of 4 x 3.25mm (US 3) dpns
- Thin cardboard
- 9 x 5cm (3½ x 2in) of 2.5cm (1in) deep foam
- Sharp darning needle
- Toy stuffing

TENSION

27 sts and 35 rows = 10cm (4in) over St-st

SEAT

FRONT

With 3.25mm (US 3) needles and MC, cast on 22 sts. Cont in moss-st until work measures 2.5cm (1in), ending on a RS. K 1 row.

TOP AND SIDES

Next row (RS): Cast on 7 sts with MC, moss-st 7 MC, **(k1, *k1, sl1 p'wise, k1, yo, psso k st and yo, k1;

rep to last st, k1) in CC** (29 sts).
Next row: Cast on 7 sts with MC, moss-st 7 MC, p22 CC, moss-st 7 MC (36 sts).
Next row: Moss-st 7 MC, rep from ** to **, moss-st 7 MC.
Rep last 2 rows until work measures 7.5cm (3in), ending on a WS. Break CC and cont in MC.

BACK
Next row (RS): Cast off 7 sts, k22, moss-st 7 (29 sts).
Next row: Cast off 7 sts, k22 (22 sts).
Cont in moss-st until work measures 10cm (4in).

BASE
Cont in St-st until work measures 15cm (6in). Cast off.

LEGS (MAKE 4)
With 2 x 3.25mm (US 3) dpns and MC, cast on 1 st.
Next row: (K1, p1, k1) into st (3 sts).
Next row: K.
Next row: Kfb to end (6 sts). Distribute sts evenly over 3 dpns (2 sts per needle) and cont in the rnd. Cont to k every rnd until work measures 2.5cm (1in).
Next rnd: (Kfb, k1) to end (9 sts). Cont to k every rnd until work measures 3.75cm (1½in).

MAKING UP
Press Seat and Back on WS using a warm iron over a damp cloth.
Make up the legs by cutting a piece of cardboard approx. 6.25 x 3.75cm (2½ x 1½in) and coiling it tightly into a small cone shape. Insert the cone into the Leg. Pin the stool seat base securely to the foam base. Mark out on the Base where you would like to place each Leg. Sew Leg to the Base with a darning needle, making sure you sew right through to the top of the foam. Place a small amount of toy stuffing on the top of the seat foam. Fold the knitted Seat piece around the foam, then pin the cast-off edge to the cast-on edge. Sew the sides to the Base. Sew the cast-on edges of the Sides to the Front to form a box. Adjust the stuffing if necessary. Sew the pinned cast-on and cast-off edges together. Darn in ends.

CURTAINS

MATERIALS
- 2 x 50g balls DMC Natura Just Cotton (100% cotton; 50g/170yds) in shade N12 Light Green (A)
- 1 x 50g ball DMC Natura Just Cotton (100% cotton; 50g/170yds) in each of shades N79 Tilleul (B), N20 Jade (C) and N43 Gold Lemon (D)
- Pair of 3.25mm (US 3) needles
- Length of dowel rod to fit desired width of window (for curtain rail)

TENSION
26 sts and 35 rows = 10cm (4in) over St-st

PATTERN NOTE: These curtains were made to fit a suggested window size of 22cm (8¾in) (W) x 54.5cm (21½in) (L). Please adapt to suit your own requirements.

MAIN CURTAINS (MAKE 2)
With B, cast on 55 sts.
Row 1 (RS): K1, *yo, k1, s2kp, k1, yo, k1, rep from * to end.
Row 2: P.
Rep these 2 rows until work measures 5cm (2in). Break B, change to C, work 2 rows in St-st. Break C, change to A. Work 2 rows in St-st, then proceed as follows:
Row 1 (RS): Sl1, k6, *sl1 p'wise, k1, yo, psso both sl and k st, k6; rep from * to end.
Row 2: Sl1, p to end.
Rep these 2 rows until work measures 40.5cm (16in) or desired length. Cast off.

BOTTOM PELMET
With C, cast on 57 sts. Work 3 rows in St-st. Change to A.
Row 1 (RS): K.
Rows 2 and 4: P.
Row 3: *(K2tog) 3 times, k1, (yo, k1) 6 times, (k2tog) 3 times; rep from * to end.
Rep rows 1–4 three times. Break A, change to C. K 2 rows, p 1 row, k 1 row. Break C, change to B. Cont in St-st until work measures 17.75cm (7in) or desired length. Cast off.

TOP PELMET
With C, cast on 57 sts.
Row 1 (RS): K1, yo, *k5, sl the 2nd, 3rd, 4th and 5th sts over first st, yo; rep from * to last st, k1.
Row 2: P1, *(p1, yo, k1 tbl) in yo, p1; rep from * to end.

Row 3: K2, k1 tbl, *k3, k1 tbl; rep from * to last 2 sts, k1.

Row 4: K.

Change to B, cont in St-st until work measures 9cm (3½in) or desired length. Cast off.

MAKING UP

Press pieces lightly on WS using a warm iron over a damp cloth, applying a little starch to give the fabric some weight. Sew a hidden running st vertically along the centre of the Top Pelmet, stopping before you reach the cast-off edge to retain a straight edge. Gather and secure.

Make small tassels with D as follows: Cut a thin piece of cardboard approx. 5cm (2in) wide x 2.5cm (1in) deep. Cut a single length of yarn approx. 10cm (4in) long and position across the width of the cardboard near the top. Wrap a few strands of yarn around the cardboard (so that they lie across the single length). Tie the single length of yarn into a knot twice tightly and remove the wraps from the cardboard. Break yarn and position the knot to the inside of the tassel. Wrap another piece of yarn or sewing thread around the tassel near the top and secure. Cut

the ends and trim neatly. Make 15 and sew them at intervals to the spaces in between the picot edging of the Top Pelmet.

Fold the cast-off edges of the Bottom and Top Pelmets over the dowel rod or wire and sew lightly. Sew a running st along the cast-off edge of the Main Curtains and gather slightly to fit the window size. Sew them to the Bottom Pelmet so that they meet in the middle. With C, make a couple of plaits to hold the curtains back, and trim with 2 tassels made with D.

OTHER ITEMS FROM THE SCENE

WENTWORTH'S TAILCOAT
Follow instructions for Darcy's Tailcoat on page 33.

WENTWORTH'S TROUSERS
See page 16. Use yarn option 3.

WENTWORTH'S BOOTS
See page 17. Use yarn option 1.

WENTWORTH'S WAISTCOAT
See page 18. Use yarn option 2.

WENTWORTH'S SHIRT
See page 17. Use yarn option 1.

ANNE'S SHOES
See page 19.

Sir Thomas Interrupts Rehearsals

MANSFIELD PARK

'How is the consternation of the party to be described?
To the greater number it was a moment of absolute horror.'

Things look happy enough for Fanny Price here as she sits watching Mary Crawford and her affectionate friend Edmund rehearse for a play, but in fact she's caught in an awkward situation. The mistress of Mansfield Park is her mother's sister, Lady Bertram, who landed quite a catch in Sir Thomas, unlike Fanny's own mother. Fanny's father is the archetypal drunken sailor and the family lives in poverty. With an ever-growing brood, Mrs Price asks her wealthy sister for help, and Fanny, a sweet-natured girl who ends up on the sharp end of her female cousins' cruel tongues, moves to Mansfield Park. Fortunately, cousin Edmund is kind and the two form a close bond.

Along come the charming siblings Mary and Henry Crawford to upset the apple cart. Shallow and calculating, Mary seems interested in the eldest Bertram son, Tom, but soon directs her attentions towards Edmund. Henry is interested in Maria, Edmund's betrothed sister. Tom suggests they put on a play called *Lovers' Vows*. Edmund and Fanny disapprove and, at first, refuse to participate, but Edmund reluctantly takes part, meaning Fanny has to painfully endure watching Mary and Edmund rehearsing intimate scenes.

When Sir Thomas returns home, he is not best pleased to discover the rehearsal, finding himself '*bewildered in his own house, making part of a ridiculous exhibition in the midst of theatrical nonsense.*' By the end of the book the mischievous souls get their comeuppance, and Edmund marries Fanny.

FANNY'S DRESS

MATERIALS

- 1 x 50g ball Scheepjeswol Cotton 8 (100% cotton; 50g/185yds) in each of shades 657 Dark Brown (A) and 659 Light Brown (B)
- Small amount of cream cotton 4ply (fingering) yarn (C)
- Pair of 3.25mm (US 3) needles

TENSION

28 sts and 36 rows = 10cm (4in) over patt

BACK and FRONT (BOTH ALIKE)

With A, cast on 52 sts. K 2 rows.
Row 1 (RS): Using B, k1, *sl2 wyib, k2; rep from * to last 3 sts, sl2 wyib, k1.
Row 2: Using B, p1, *sl2 wyif, p2; rep from * to last 3 sts, sl2 wyif, p1.
Row 3: Using A, k1, *k2, sl2 wyib; rep from * to last 3 sts, k3.
Row 4: Using B, p1, *p2, sl2 wyif; rep from * to last 3 sts, p3.

Rep these 4 rows until work measures 16.5cm (6½in), ending on a WS.
Next row: With A, k2tog to end (26 sts).
Next row: With A, p to end.
Cont in patt as follows:
Row 1 (RS): Using B, k1, *k1, sl1 wyib; rep from * to last st, k1.
Row 2: Using B, *p1, sl1 wyif; rep from * to last 2 sts, p2.
Row 3: With A, *k1, sl1 wyib; rep from * to last 2 sts, k2.
Row 4: Using A, p1, *p1, sl1 wyif; rep from * to end.
Rep these 4 rows once more, at the same time inc 1 st at each end of 3rd row (28 sts). Work Rows 1–2 once more.

Armhole

Cast off 2 sts at each end of next 2 rows (24 sts). Cont without shaping until Armhole measures 2.5cm (1in), ending on a WS.
Next row: Work 6 sts, turn. Cont working in patt on these 6 sts for left shoulder. Cont without shaping until Armhole measures 4.5cm (1¾in). Cast off. With RS facing, using C, rejoin yarn to rem 18 sts. K12 sts, turn. K 1 row. Cast off the 12 sts.
With RS facing, rejoin A and B to rem 6 sts for right shoulder. Cont without shaping until Armhole measures 4.5cm (1¾in). Cast off.

SLEEVES (MAKE 2)

With A, cast on 18 sts. K 2 rows.
Row 1 (RS): Using B, *k1, sl1 wyib; rep from * to last 2 sts, k2.
Row 2: Using B, p2, *sl1 wyif, p1; rep from * to end.
Row 3: Using A, k1, *k1, sl1 wyib, k1; rep from * to last st, k1.
Row 4: Using A, *p1, sl1 wyif; rep from * to last 2 sts, p2.
Rep these 4 rows until work measures 11.5cm (4½in), at the same time inc 1 st at each end of every 10th row to 30 sts.
Cast off 2 sts at each end of next and every foll 3rd row until 16 sts rem. Dec 1 st at each end of next and every foll alt row until 8 sts rem. Cast off.

MAKING UP

Press lightly on WS using a warm iron over a damp cloth. Sew shoulder and side seams. Sew sleeve seams and sew into armholes, gathering slightly at top if necessary. Sew in cream neck band at sides. Sew a running st around waist, gather and secure to fit the doll. Darn in ends.

MARY'S DRESS

Follow instructions for Emma's Dress on page 54, adding this Frill.

MATERIALS

- 1 x 50g ball Wendy Merino 4ply (fingering 100% wool; 50g/191yds) in shade 2365 Birch
- Pair of 3.25mm (US 3) needles

DRESS FRILL

Cast on 67 sts.
Row 1 (RS): K2, *yo, k2, s2kp, k2, yo, k1; rep from * to last st, k1.
Row 2: P.
These 2 rows form the patt. Work in patt 3 more times.
Next row (RS): K1, k2tog; rep to last st, k1 (45 sts).
K 2 rows. Cast off.

Sir Thomas' Striped Waistcoat

MATERIALS
- 1 x 50g ball Adriafil Azzurra (70% wool/30% acrylic; 50g/246yds) in each of shades 070 Mélange Anthracite Grey (MC) and 48 Light Mélange Grey (CC)
- Pair of 3.25mm (US 3) needles
- 3 small beads

TENSION
28 sts and 32 rows = 10cm (4in) over patt

BACK
With MC, cast on 40 sts. K 2 rows.
Row 1 (RS): Using CC, k1, *sl2 wyib, k2; rep from * to last 3 sts, sl2 wyib, k1.
Row 2: Using CC, k1, *sl2 wyif, p2; rep from * to last 3 sts, sl2 wyif, k1.
Row 3: Using MC, k1, *k2, sl2 wyib; rep from * to last 3 sts, k3.
Row 4: With MC, k1, *p2, sl2 wyif; rep to last 3 sts, p2, k1.
Rep these 4 rows until work measures 6.25cm (2½in), ending on a RS.

Armhole
Cont in patt, cast off 2 sts at beg of next 2 rows (36 sts). Dec 1 st at each end of next and foll alt row (32 sts). Cont in patt without shaping until Armhole measures 6.25cm (2½in). Cast off.

RIGHT FRONT
Cast on 25 sts with MC. K 2 rows.
Row 1 (RS): K3MC, *k2CC, k2MC; rep to last 2 sts, k2CC.
Row 2: *P2CC, p2MC; rep from * to last 5 sts, p2CC, k3MC.
Rep these last 2 rows until work measures 6.25cm (2½in), ending on a RS.

Armhole
Cast off 2 sts at beg of next row, patt to end (23 sts).
Next row: K4MC, patt to last 2 sts, k2tog (22 sts).
Next row: Patt to last 4 sts, k4MC.
Next row: K5MC, patt to last 2 sts, k2tog (21 sts).
Next row: Patt to last 5 sts, k5MC.
Next row: K6MC, patt to end.
Cont in this manner, inc 1 extra MC k st at the outer edge to create a lapel, until you have worked 11 k sts in MC, ending on a RS.
Next row: Cast off 10 sts, k to end.
Cont in garter-st on rem 11 sts for back collar for another 2cm (¾in). Cast off.

LEFT FRONT
Repeat instructions for Right Front, reversing shapings and lapel instructions.

MAKING UP
Press pieces lightly on WS using a warm iron over a damp cloth. Sew shoulders and side seams. Sew cast-off edges of back collar. Sew back collar to the neck back. Overlap the front edges and sew. Attach three small beads evenly along the front edge for buttons. Darn in ends.

Sir Thomas' Riding Coat

MATERIALS
- 1 x 50g ball Adriafil Azzurra (70% wool/30% acrylic; 50g/246yds) in shade 070 Mélange Anthracite Grey
- Pair of 3.25mm (US 3) needles

TENSION
28 sts and 40 rows = 10cm (4in) over St-st

Follow instructions for Darcy's coat on page 47, with this addition:

CAPE
Cast on 21 sts. Work 2 rows in moss-st.
Row 1 (RS): K1, p1, k to last 2 sts, p1, k1.
Row 2: K1, p1, p15, w&t.
Row 3: K to last 2 sts, p1, k1.
Row 4: K1, p1, k1, p to last 3 sts, k1, p1, k1.
Rep these 4 rows until shortest edge of work measures 15cm (6in). Work 2 rows in moss-st. Cast off.

MAKING UP
Press pieces lightly on WS using a warm iron over a damp cloth. Follow instructions for Darcy's coat. To attach the Cape, gather if necessary at the shortest edge to fit the neckline of the coat. Sew to secure. Darn in ends.

EDMUND'S WAISTCOAT

MATERIALS

- 100g ball DMC Petra 3 (100% cotton; 100g/306yds) in shade 5712 Beige
- Pair of 3.25mm (US 3) needles
- 3 small beads

TENSION

28 sts and 36 rows = 10cm (4in) in St-st

BACK

Cast on 32 sts.

Row 1 (RS): *K1, sl1 p'wise wyif; rep from * to end.

Rows 2 and 4: P.

Row 3: *Sl1 p'wise wyif, k1; rep from * to end.

Cont to rep these 4 rows to form st patt until work measures 5cm (2in).

Armhole

Cast off 2 sts at beg next 2 rows (28 sts). Dec 1 st at each end of next and foll alt row (24 sts). Cont in patt until Armhole measures 6.25cm (2½in). Cast off.

RIGHT FRONT

Cast on 20 sts. Work in st patt until work measures 5cm (2in), ending on a RS.

Armhole

Cast off 2 sts at beg next row (18 sts). Dec 1 st at end of next and foll alt row (16 sts). Cont in patt until

Armhole measures 6.25cm (2½in), at the same time dec 1 st at neck edge on every foll 7th row until 13 sts rem ending on a RS.

Next row: Cast off 7 sts for shoulder, patt to end. To form Back Collar, cont in patt st on rem 6 sts until Collar measures 2.5cm (1in). Cast off.

LEFT FRONT

Follow instructions for Right Front, reversing shapings.

MAKING UP

Press all pieces lightly on WS using a warm iron over a damp cloth. Sew shoulder and side seams. Join back collar seams and sew to Back. Attach small beads to Left Front button band, overlapping the Left Front over the Right slightly and securing the Fronts so that they are attached. Darn in ends.

CAT

MATERIALS

- 1 x 50g ball Adriafil Azzurra (70% wool/30% acrylic; 50g/246yds) in each of shades 48 Light Mélange Grey (MC) and 11 Cream (CC)
- Small amount of pink 4ply yarn for nose

- Small amount of blue 4ply yarn for eyes
- Pair of 2.75mm (US 2) needles
- Set of 4 x 2.75mm (US 2) dpns
- Small amount of toy stuffing
- Small length of armature wire or pipe cleaner for tail

HEAD

With CC, cast on 3 sts.

Row 1 (RS): Kfb to end (6 sts). Distribute evenly over 3 dpns (2 sts per needle) and work in the rnd.

Rnd 2: K.

Rnd 3: K1, kfb; rep to end (9 sts).

Rnd 4: K.

Rnd 5: K1, (k2tog) twice, k1, kfb, k1, kfb (9 sts).

Rnd 6: (Kfb) 4 times, (k1, kfb) twice, k1 (15 sts).

Rnd 7: (Kfb twice, k1) in CC, k2 MC, (k1, [kfb twice]) in CC, ([k1, k2tog] twice, k1) in CC (17 sts).

Rnd 8: K4 CC, k4 MC, (k4, k2tog, k1, k2tog) CC (15 sts).

Rnd 9: K2 MC, k2 CC, k1 MC, (kfb MC) twice, k1 MC, k2 CC, k2 MC, k3tog CC (15 sts).

Rnd 10: K12, w&t, p10, w&t, k8, w&t, p6, w&t, k4, w&t, p2, w&t, k to end of 2nd needle, turn, p to end of 1st needle.

Break CC and cont in MC.

Rnd 11: K14, (k1, p1, k1) into last st (17 sts).

Rnd 12: K3, k2tog, k4, k2tog, k3, kfb, k1, kfb (17 sts).

Rnd 13: K2, k2tog, k4, k2tog, k to end (15 sts).

Rnd 14: K1, k2tog, k4, k2tog, k2, (kfb, k1) twice (15 sts).

Rnd 15: K.

BODY

Rnd 16: K2tog, k4, k2tog, k to end (13 sts).

Rnd 17: K.

Rnd 18: (Kfb, k1, kfb) twice, k to end (17 sts).

Rnd 19: K.

Rnd 20: (K1, kfb) twice, k2, (kfb, k1) twice, k1, kfb, k3, kfb, k1 (23 sts).

Rnd 21: K.

Rnd 22: (K2, kfb) 4 times, k2, k1, kfb, (k2, kfb) twice, k1 (30 sts).

Rnd 23: K.

Rnd 24: (K2, kfb) 3 times, (kfb, k2) 3 times, k1, kfb, (k2, kfb) 3 times, k1 (40 sts). Stuff firmly.

Rnds 25–28: K.

Rnd 29: K27, k2tog, (k3, k2tog) twice, k1 (37 sts).

Rnd 30: K.

Rnd 31: (K2, k2tog) twice, k8, (k2tog, k2) twice, (k3, k2tog) twice, k3 (31 sts).

Rnds 32–34: K.

Rnd 35: K3, k2tog, k1, k2tog, k4, k2tog, k1, k2tog, k5, k2tog, k3, k2tog, k2 (25 sts).

Rnds 36–38: K.

Rnd 39: K14, w&t, p12, w&t, k10, w&t, p8, w&t, k to end of 2nd needle, turn, p to end of 1st needle.

Rnd 40: (K2, k2tog, k1, k2tog) twice, k4, k2tog, k1, k2tog, k2 (19 sts). Stuff firmly.

Rnd 41: K.

Rnd 42: (K1, k2tog) twice, (k2tog, k1) twice, (k1, k2tog) twice, k1 (13 sts).

Rnd 43: K.

Rnd 44: K1, k2tog, k2, k2tog, (k1, k2tog) twice (9 sts). Stuff firmly if necessary.

TAIL

Cont to k rnds until Tail measures 4.5cm (1¾in).

Next rnd: K1, (k2tog) twice, k to end (7 sts). Cont to k rnds until Tail measures 5.75cm (2¼in). Insert a small piece of wire and some stuffing into tail.

Next rnd: (K2tog) twice, k3tog (3 sts). Break yarn and draw end through rem sts.

BACK LEGS (MAKE 2)

With CC, cast on 3 sts.

Row 1 (RS): Kfb to end (6 sts). Distribute sts evenly over 3 dpns (2 sts per needle) and cont to work in the rnd.

Rnd 2: K.

Rnd 3: (K1, kfb) 3 times (9 sts). K 10 rnds. Stuff firmly.

Next rnd: (K2tog, k1) to end (6 sts).

Next rnd: K2tog to end (3 sts). Break yarn and draw end through rem sts.

FRONT LEGS (MAKE 2)

With CC, cast on 3 sts.

Row 1 (RS): Kfb to end (6 sts). Distribute evenly over 3 dpns (2 sts per needle) and cont working in the rnd.

Rnds 2–3: K.

Rnd 4: K1, kfb, k to end (7 sts).

Rnds 5–6: K.

Rnd 7: K3, turn, p3, k3, p3.

Rnds 8–11: K.

Break CC and cont to work in MC. K until work measures 2.5cm (1in) from point where MC was joined. Stuff firmly.

Next rnd: K2tog, k1, (k2tog) twice (4 sts).

Next rnd: K2tog twice (2 sts). Break yarn and draw end through rem sts.

MAKING UP

Position the Back Legs underneath the Body in the appropriate position and sew to secure. Sew a couple of sts in the Tail to secure it to the Body in desired position. Position the Front Legs to the front sides of the Body and sew to secure. Mark out on the Head where you would like to position the ears. Using 2.75mm (US 2) needles and MC, pick up 5 sts from desired position of Head. K 2 rows. Dec 1 st at each end of foll 2 rows (1 st). Break yarn and draw through end of rem st.

Embroider a small pink nose. Mark out where you would like to place the eyes and sew a small French knot (see page 108) in each spot. Thread 3 strands of cream yarn through the nose for whiskers, and trim to desired length. Darn in ends.

RUG

MATERIALS

- 1 x 50g ball Patons Diploma Gold 4ply (fingering 55% wool/25% acrylic/20% nylon; 50g/201yds) in each of shades 4239 Cherry (MC) and 4282 Cream (CC)
- Pair of 3.25mm (US 3) needles
- Set of 4 x 3.25mm (US 3) dpns

With MC, cast on 49 sts. Work 4 rows in moss-st.

Next row (RS): (K1, p1, k1) in MC, k with CC to last 3 sts, (k1, p1, k1) in MC.

Next row: (K1, p1, k1) in MC, p with CC to last 3 sts, (k1, p1, k1) in MC.

Cont in main patt as follows:

Row 1 (RS): (K1, p1, k1) in MC, k2 CC, cont in MC, k1, sl1 wyif, k1, *sl1 wyib, k1, sl1 wyif, k1; rep from * to last 5 sts, k2 CC, (1, p1, k1) in MC.

Row 2 (K1, p1, k1) in MC, p2 CC, cont in MC, p3, *sl1 wyif, p3; rep from * to last 5 sts, p2 CC, (k1, p1, k1) in MC.

Row 3: (K1, p1, k1) in MC, k2 CC, cont in CC, k1, *sl1 wyif, k3; rep from * to last 7 sts, sl1 wyif, k1, k2 CC, (k1, p1, k1) in MC.

Row 4: (K1, p1, k1) in MC, p2 CC, cont in CC, p to last 5 sts, p2 CC, (k1, p1, k1) in MC.

Row 5: (K1, p1, k1) in MC, k2 CC, cont in MC, k1, sl1 wyib, k1, *sl1 wyif, k1, sl1 wyib, k1; rep from * to last 5 sts, k2 CC, (k1, p1, k1) in MC.

Row 6: (K1, p1, k1) in MC, p2 CC, cont in MC, p1, *sl1 wyif, p3; rep from * to last 7 sts, sl1 wyib, p1, p2 CC, (k1, p1, k1) in MC.

Row 7: (K1, p1, k1) in MC, k2 CC, cont in CC, k3, *sl1 wyif, k3; rep from * to last 5 sts, k2 CC, (k1, p1, k1) in MC.

Row 8: (K1, p1, k1) in MC, p2 CC, cont in CC, p to last 5 sts, p2 CC, (k1, p1, k1) in MC.

Rep these 8 rows of patt until work measures approx. 20cm (8in), ending on a Row 8.

Next row (RS): (K1, p1, k1) in MC, k with CC to last 3 sts, (k1, p1, k1) in MC.

Next row: (K1, p1, k1) in MC, p with CC to last 3 sts, (k1, p1, k1) in MC.

Next row: (K1, p1, k1) in MC, k with CC to last 3 sts, (k1, p1, k1) in MC. Break CC.

Next row: Cont in MC, k1, p1, k1, p to last 3 sts, k1, p1, k1.

Moss-st 4 rows in MC. Cast off.

MAKING UP

Press on WS using a warm iron over a damp cloth. Darn in ends.

OTHER ITEMS FROM THE SCENE

Sir Thomas' Trousers
See page 16. Use yarn option 1.

Sir Thomas' Shirt
See page 17. Use yarn option 3.

Sir Thomas' Boots
See page 17. Use yarn option 1.

Edmund's Breeches
See page 16. Use yarn option 3.

Edmund's Shirt
See page 17. Use yarn option 1.

Edmund's Boots
See page 17. Use yarn option 2.

Ladies' Shoes
See page 19.

CATHERINE IS CAUGHT SNOOPING

NORTHANGER ABBEY

*'Dear Miss Morland, consider the dreadful nature
of the suspicions you have entertained.'*

Catherine Morland has been getting carried away with reading far too many Gothic novels. That, of course, would account for how she finds herself rifling through a dead lady's belongings in a locked chamber.

During a stay in Bath, the impressionable seventeen-year-old Catherine is invited to spend time with the Tilney siblings, including the clergyman Mr Henry Tilney. They visit the Tilney family home, and Catherine's overactive imagination is piqued when she hears the name of their dwelling: *'Northanger Abbey! These were thrilling words, and wound up Catherine's feelings to the highest point of ecstasy.'* The appearance of the place, however, doesn't quite live up to her fevered imaginings.

On hearing that the general's wife passed away, Catherine becomes convinced that the general murdered his wife and decides to investigate the deceased lady's room. Far from the terrifying scenes described in *The Mysteries of Udolpho*, she finds herself in a perfectly ordinary room (bar the odd spider). As she realises her folly, she is discovered by Henry Tilney. It gradually dawns on Henry what has been going on in Catherine's head; he sharply pulls her back into the world of reason: *'Consult your own understanding, your own sense of the probable, your own observation of what is passing around you.'* It turns out that there are no suspicious circumstances surrounding Mrs Tilney's death. An ashamed Catherine runs back to her room in tears, which doesn't bode well for her and Henry's relationship, but despite this and General Tilney's initial financial objections, Henry and Catherine end up man and wife.

CATHERINE'S SHAWL

MATERIALS

Yarn in the following options:
- 1 x 100g ball Drops Lace (30% silk/70% alpaca; 100g/191yds) in shade 7120 Light Grey Green

OR

- Small amount of similar 2ply (laceweight) yarn
- Pair of 3.25mm (US 3) needles

Cast on 3 sts.

Row 1 (RS): K1, yo, k1, yo, k1 (5 sts).

Row 2 (and all foll even rows): K.

Row 3: K1, yo, k3, yo, k1 (7 sts).

Row 5: K1, yo, k5, yo, k1 (9 sts).

Row 7: K1, yo, k7, yo, k1 (11 sts).

Row 9: K1, yo, k9, yo, k1 (13 sts).

Row 11: (K1, yo) twice, k3, k3tog tbl, k3, (yo, k1) twice (15 sts).

Row 13: K1, yo, k3, yo, k2, k3tog tbl, k2, yo, k3, yo, k1 (17 sts).

Row 15: K1, yo, k5, yo, k1, k3tog tbl, k1, yo, k5, yo, k1 (19 sts).

Row 17: K1, yo, k7, yo, k3tog tbl, yo, k7, yo, k1 (21 sts).

Row 19: K1, yo, k2, ssk, yo, k1, yo, k3, k3tog tbl, k3, yo, k1, yo, k2tog, k2, yo, k1 (23 sts).

Row 21: K1, yo, k2, ssk, yo, k3, yo, k2, k3tog tbl, k2, yo, k3, yo, k2tog, k2, yo, k1 (25 sts).

Row 23: K1, yo, k2, ssk, yo, k5, yo, k1, k3tog tbl, k1, yo, k5, yo, k2tog, k2, yo, k1 (27 sts).

Row 25: (K1, yo) twice, k3tog tbl, yo, k7, yo, k3tog tbl, yo, k7, yo, k3tog tbl, (yo, k1) twice (29 sts).

Row 27: K1, yo, k3, ssk, k3, yo, k1, yo, k3, k3tog tbl, k3, yo, k1, yo, k3, k2tog, k3, yo, k1 (31 sts).

Row 29: (K1, yo) twice, k2, k3tog tbl, k2, yo, k3, yo, k2, k3tog tbl, k2, yo, k3, yo, k2, k3tog tbl, k2, (yo, k1) twice (33 sts).

Row 31: K1, yo, k3, yo, k1, k3tog tbl, k1, yo, k5, yo, k1, k3tog tbl, k1, yo, k5, yo, k1, k3tog tbl, k1, yo, k3, yo, k1 (35 sts).

Row 33: K1, yo, k5, yo, k3tog tbl, yo, k7, yo, k3tog tbl, yo, k7, yo, k3tog tbl, yo, k5, yo, k1 (37 sts).

Row 35: K1, yo, k3, yo, k3, k3tog tbl, k3, yo, k1, yo, k3, k3tog tbl, k3, yo, k1, yo, k3, k3tog tbl, (k3, yo) twice, k1 (39 sts).

Row 37: K1, yo, k5, yo, k2, k3tog tbl, k2, yo, k3, yo, k2, k3tog tbl, k2, yo, k3, yo, k2, k3tog tbl, k2, yo, k5, yo, k1 (41 sts).

Row 39: K1, yo, k7, yo, k1, k3tog tbl, k1, yo, k5, yo, k1, k3tog tbl, k1, yo, k5, yo, k1, k3tog tbl, k1, yo, k7, yo, k1 (43 sts).

Row 41: K1, yo, k9, yo, k3tog tbl, yo, k7, yo, k3tog tbl, yo, k7, yo, k3tog tbl, yo, k9, yo, k1 (45 sts).

Row 43: K1, yo, k4, ssk, yo, k1, yo, k3, k3tog tbl, k3, yo, k1, yo, k3, k3tog tbl, k3, yo, k1, yo, k2tog, k4, yo, k1 (47 sts).

Row 45: K1, yo, k4, ssk, yo, k3, yo, k2, k3tog tbl, k2, yo, k3, yo, k2, k3tog tbl, k2, yo, k3, yo, k2, k3tog tbl, k2, yo, k3, yo, k2tog, k4, yo, k1 (49 sts).

Row 47: (K1, yo) twice, k1, k3tog tbl, k1, yo, k5, yo, k1, k3tog tbl, k1, yo, k5, yo, k1, k3tog tbl, k1, yo, k5, yo, k1, k3tog tbl, (k1, yo) twice, k1 (51 sts).

Row 49: K1, yo, k3, yo, k3tog tbl, yo, k7, yo, k3tog tbl, yo, k7, yo, k3tog tbl, yo, k7, yo, k3tog tbl, yo, k3, yo, k1 (53 sts).

Row 51: (K1, yo) twice, k3, k3tog tbl, k3, yo, k1, yo, k3, k3tog tbl, k3, yo, k1, yo, k3, k3tog tbl, k3, yo, k1, yo, k3, k3tog tbl, k3, (yo, k1) twice (55 sts).

Row 53: K1, yo, k3, yo, k2, k3tog tbl, k2, yo, k3, yo, k2, k3tog tbl, k2, yo, k3, yo, k2, k3tog tbl, k2, yo, k3, yo, k2, k3tog tbl, k2, yo, k3, yo, k2, k3tog tbl, k2, yo, k3, yo, k1 (57 sts).

Row 55: K1, yo, k5, yo, k1, k3tog tbl, k1, yo, k5, yo, k1, k3tog tbl, k1, yo, k5, yo, k1, k3tog tbl, k1, yo, k5, yo, k1, k3tog tbl, k1, yo, k5, yo, k1 (59 sts).

Row 57: K1, yo, k7, yo, k3tog tbl, yo, k7, yo, k3tog tbl, yo, k7, yo, k3tog tbl, yo, k7, yo, k3tog tbl, yo, k7, yo, k1 (61 sts).

Cast off.

MAKING UP

Press lightly on WS using a warm iron over a damp cloth. Darn in ends.

HENRY'S WAISTCOAT

MATERIALS

- 1 x 50g ball Rowan Pure Wool 4ply (fingering 100% wool; 50g/174yds) in shade 461 Ochre
- Pair of 3.25mm (US 3) needles
- 3 small beads

TENSION

27 sts and 37 rows = 10cm (4in) over St-st

BACK

Cast on 33 sts. Work 2 rows in moss-st. Cont without shaping in St-st until work measures 5cm (2in), ending on a WS.

Armhole
Cast off 2 sts at beg of next 2 rows (29 sts). Dec 1 st at each end of next and foll alt row (25 sts). Cont without shaping until Armhole measures 6.25cm (2½in).
Next row (RS): Cast off 8 sts, work 9 sts in moss-st, cast off 8 sts. Break yarn.
With RS facing, rejoin yarn to rem 9 sts. Work 5 rows in moss-st. Cast off.

LEFT FRONT

Cast on 19 sts. Work 2 rows in moss-st.
Next row (RS): K to last 2 sts, p1, k1.
Next row: K1, p1, k1, p to end.
Cont without shaping in St-st with moss-st button band until work measures 5cm (2in), ending on a WS.

Armhole
Cast off 2 sts at beg of next row (17 sts). Patt 1 row.
Next row (RS): K2tog, k to last 4 sts, (p1, k1) twice (16 sts).
Next row: K1, p1, k1, p to end.
Next row: K2tog, k to last 4 sts, (p1, k1) twice (15 sts).
Next row: (K1, p1) twice, k1, p to end.

Next row: K to last 6 sts, (p1, k1) 3 times.
Next row: (K1, p1) twice, k1, p to end.
Rep last 2 rows twice.
Next row: K to last 8 sts, (p1, k1) 4 times.
Next row: (K1, p1) 4 times, p to end.
Next row: Cast off 7 sts (8 sts). Cont in moss-st on rem 8 sts for 5 rows. Cast off.

RIGHT FRONT

Follow instructions for Left Front, reversing shapings.

MAKING UP

Press all pieces lightly on WS using a warm iron over a damp cloth. Sew shoulder and continuation collar seams. Sew side seams and attach small beads to Left Front button band, overlapping the Left Front over the Right slightly and securing the Fronts so that they are attached. Darn in ends.

HENRY'S BREECHES

MATERIALS

- 1 x 100g ball DMC Petra 3 (100% cotton; 100g/306yds) in shade 5712
- Pair of 2.75mm (US 2) needles
- Pair of 3.25mm (US 3) needles

TENSION

25 sts and 38 rows = 10cm (4in) over St-st

See page 16.

HENRY'S SHIRT

MATERIALS

- 2 x 25g ball Jamieson & Smith 2ply 2ply (laceweight, 100% Shetland wool; 25g/125yds) in shade 01A (Cream)
- Pair of 3.25mm (US 3) needles

TENSION

28 sts and 37 rows = 10cm (4in) over St-st

Follow instructions for Brandon's Shirt on page 82.

HENRY'S BOOTS

MATERIALS
- 1 x 50g ball Scheepjeswol Cotton 80 (100% cotton; 50g/295yds) in shade 657 Dark Brown
- Pair of 3.25mm (US 3) needles
- Small amount of thin cardboard

See page 17.

SPIDER AND COBWEB

MATERIALS
- Small amount of black yarn for Spider (MC) (fingering or sport weight)
- Small amount of white yarn (fingering or sport weight) for Cobweb (CC)
- White or paste glue

WEB
Cut 3 lengths of CC and tie them together in the middle. Pin the ends of the threads out on to a piece of foam or an ironing board to form the main web structure. Thread a darning needle with a long length of CC, then create outer circles of web, tying them to the main structure as you go. Using a paintbrush, paste the entire web with glue to ensure a stiff structure.

SPIDER
With MC, make a small pom-pom, leaving a long length of yarn for the hanging thread. Trim the pom-pom to the desired size. To make the legs, cut 4 lengths of MC and thread them through the centre of the Spider's body at even intervals, leaving an equal amount of thread hanging at either side. Trim to desired length. To make the eyes, thread through a length of CC near the front of the pom-pom. Tie a knot at one end and pull through so that it is flush to the pom-pom surface. Tie a knot in the other end close to the surface to form the second eye. Trim ends. Attach the Spider to the Web with the hanging thread.

OTHER ITEMS FROM THE SCENE

BASKET
See instructions for Picnic Basket on page 63, omitting plate.

Extra techniques

I-CORD

A knitted tubular cord, created with two dpns:

1. Cast on 3 or 4 sts, according to pattern instructions. Knit 1 row. Do not turn.
2. Slide sts along the dpn back to right-hand tip of needle.

3. Swap needle to left hand, ready for the next row. Knit the sts, pulling yarn tight across the back of the sts. Do not turn.
4. Rep steps 2 and 3 until cord is desired length.
5. Cut yarn, thread through sts and pull tight.

FRENCH KNOT

1. Thread a sewing needle with one strand of yarn, or more for bigger knots.
2. Bring needle up at 1 and wrap thread once around needle.

3. Insert needle at 2, close to where it came up, holding wrapped thread taut.
4. Pass needle through the fabric, leaving the knot on the surface.

POM-POM

1. Cut two doughnut-shaped rings from stiff cardboard and hold together.
2. Wind yarn firmly around cardboard rings through the hole, until it is almost filled.
3. Using sharp scissors, cut yarn strands between the cardboard layers. Do not pull the layers apart.

4. Pass a length of yarn or strong sewing thread between the layers. Pull tight and knot securely.
5. Cut a slit in each cardboard ring from the edge to centre hole. Remove cardboard and fluff out pom-pom.

GRAFTING (KITCHENER STITCH)

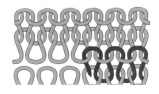

Grafting (or Kitchener stitch) is used when joining two pieces of knitting together for a seamless join. In order to join the pieces together, the stitches to be grafted need to be left on the needle. The pieces are grafted from right to left. The following example uses stocking stitch as the primary stitch, which is what is used for the hood in Lydia's Cape on page 40.

1. Insert darning needle knitwise through first stitch on front knitting needle, draw yarn through and slip the stitch off the knitting needle.

2. Insert needle purlwise through second stitch on front knitting needle, draw yarn through but leave the stitch on the needle.
3. Insert needle purlwise through the first stitch on back knitting needle, draw yarn through and slip the stitch off.
4. Insert needle knitwise through the second stitch on back knitting needle, leaving the stitch on the needle. Repeat steps 1–4.

FRINGE

1. Wind yarn several times around a piece of cardboard, which should be the desired length of your fringe; you can make it longer than necessary and trim. Cut the yarn.
2. With RS of fabric facing, insert a crochet hook from the WS, fold two pieces of cut yarn in half, wind them around the hook and pull through to the fabric WS, creating a loop on the WS.

3. With the hook still in the loop, hook the loose ends of the yarn from the RS all the way through the loop and pull firmly (but not too tightly). Continue in this manner along the edge at even intervals. Trim as desired.

DUPLICATE STITCH

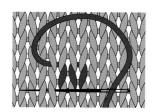

1. Thread a blunt darning needle with yarn and secure at back of fabric.
2. Bring needle from back to front at base of stitch to be covered and draw yarn through.
3. Insert needle behind the 2 loops of stitch above from right to left and draw yarn through.

4. Insert needle into base of stitch again and bring up at base of next stitch to be covered.
5. Draw yarn through loosely so sts lie on top of knitting. Continue in this way until entire motif is embroidered.

FINISHING TECHNIQUES

ARMCHAIR
(Continued from page 28)

MAKING UP

Press Seat and Back on WS using a warm iron over a damp cloth. With C and B, add the motifs according to the chart using Swiss darning. Make up the legs by cutting a piece of cardboard approx. 6.25 x 10cm (2½ x 4in) and coiling it tightly into a small cone shape. Insert the cone into the leg. Pin the chair Seat Base securely to the foam base. Mark out on the Base where you would like to place each Leg. Sew Leg to the Base with a sharp darning needle, making sure you sew right through to the top of the foam. Cut a piece of armature or florist's wire approx. 20cm (8in) long and fold in half. Insert both ends of the wire through the top of the foam so that it goes right down into the Leg (you should have a small 'loop' on the top of the foam). This secures the Leg to make it more stable. Repeat for each Leg. Place a small amount of toy stuffing on the top of the Seat foam, covering the small wire loops. Fold the knitted Seat piece around the foam, then pin the cast-off edge to the cast-on edge. Sew the sides to the Base. Sew the cast-on edges of the sides to the Front to form a box. Adjust the stuffing if necessary. Sew the pinned cast-on and cast-off edges together. Darn in ends.

Make up the Back in the same way, omitting the Leg procedure.

Position the Base of the Back on to the Seat, ensuring that the stripes match up. Sew securely.

For the cushion indents on the Seat and Back, use pins to mark 4 even points where you'd like to place them. With A, tie a knot leaving a long tail and insert the needle into the foam at the back, pulling it through to the front where your first marker is. Insert your needle at a point next to where your yarn emerged and pull it through to the back of the foam. Pull tight so that an indent is made. Fasten off and repeat. Darn in ends.

To make up the Arms, cut a piece of wire approx. 25cm (10in) in length and insert carefully into the I-cord, ensuring that it doesn't poke out of the piece. Curve into a suitable chair arm shape. Sew to the chair in the appropriate places (see photo).

ABBREVIATIONS

alt . . . . . alternate

approx . . approximately

beg . . . . . beginning

CC . . . . . contrasting colour

cm . . . . . centimetres

cont . . . . continue

dec . . . . . decrease

dpn(s) . . double-pointed needles

est . . . . . established

foll . . . . following

garter-st . garter stitch (knit every row)

g . . . . grams

inc . . . . . increase

k . . . . knit

k2tog . . . knit two together (decreases 1 stitch)

kfb . . . . . knit into front and back of next stitch (increases 1 stitch)

m . . . . . . metres

m1 . . . . . make one stitch: pick up horizontal loop between the needles and work into the back of it

m1L . . . . make a stitch by inserting your left needle into the loop lying in front of the next stitch from front to back, then knitting into the back of the stitch. Creates a '\\' shape

m1R . . . . make a stitch by inserting your left needle into the loop lying in front of the next stitch from back to front, then knitting into the front of the stitch (knitwise). Creates a '/' shape

MC . . . . . main colour

mm . . . . . millimetres

p . . . . purl

p2tog . . . purl two together decreases 1 stitch)

patt . . . . . pattern

pfb . . . . . purl into front and back of next stitch (increases 1 stitch)

psso . . . . pass slipped stitch over

p'wise . . . purlwise

rem . . . . . remaining

rep . . . . . repeat

rev St-st . reverse stocking stitch

rnd(s) . . round(s)

RS . . . . . right side

s2kp . . . . slip two, knit one, pass the slipped stitch over

sk2po . . . slip one, knit 2 together, pass the slipped stitch over

skpo . . . . slip one, knit one, pass the slipped stitch over

sl1 . . . . . . slip one stitch

ssk . . . . . slip next 2 sts, one at a time as if to knit, to the right needle. Insert left needle into fronts of these 2 stitches and k2tog

st(s) . . . . stitch(es)

St-st . . . . stocking stitch

tbl . . . . . . through back of loop

tog . . . . . together

tr . . . . treble

w&t . . . . wrap and turn (see Basic techniques, page 21)

WS . . . . . wrong side

wyib . . . . with yarn in back

wyif . . . . with yarn in front

yf . . . . . . yarn forward

yo . . . . . . yarn over

INDEX

INDEX

ACKNOWLEDGEMENTS

My eternal love and thanks as always to Roger and Lucas. Thanks to Volfie as ever for his sterling talent and enthusiasm, to Cath for her eagle eyes and keeping me in check, and to Brenda and Esther for their fantastic stitchwork. And finally, here's to the folks at RotoVision for their creativity, collaboration and for driving me into realms I hadn't previously considered.